# CUSTOMER
## *Romance*

# CUSTOMER
## *Romance*

A New Feel of Customer Service

J. N. HALM

authorHOUSE®

AuthorHouse™ UK Ltd.
1663 Liberty Drive
Bloomington, IN 47403 USA
www.authorhouse.co.uk
Phone: 0800.197.4150

Published by AuthorHouse     02/28/2014

ISBN: 978-1-4918-9678-5 (sc)
ISBN: 978-1-4918-9679-2 (e)

# CONTENTS

*"In this day and age, it is the business that knows how to woo and win the hearts of its customers that will eventually win their pockets."*

# DEDICATION

*To the love of my life, Baaba;*
*the joy of my life, Nkunim;*
*and the pride of my life, Nkosuo.*

*Everyday with you three is a lesson in love and*
*I couldn't have asked for better tutors.*

# ACKNOWLEDGEMENTS

To claim all the credit for this book would be the apex of conceit. The product you hold in your hands came to life as a result of hard work and dedication from the best team an author can ask for. I am not a self-made man and so this book cannot have been self-made.

My good friend, Mr Frank Ofori of the Treasury Department of National Investment Bank Limited of Ghana, read through the first draft of the script and made some very useful suggestions. My good friend and senior colleague in the inky fraternity, Toma Imirhe, was benevolent enough to edit the manuscript at a point. He was even gracious enough to teach me some basic English Grammar. Obviously, I am still learning.

*My Partner in Creative Insanity*, Mr Richard Bekyi of ISEEWORKS ADL, is one of the main pillars behind this project. From his constant "pestering" on when the book was coming out, the exquisite design he made for the front cover and even helping in editing the final work, he was there to the very end. I salute your priceless contribution to this project, my brother.

This book would have remained a disjointed manuscript on my *HP ProBook* had I not listened to a presentation by one of my most inspiring mentors, speaker and author, Rev. Albert Ocran. After listening to *Writers Live Twice* from the Springboard 2013 Road Show, I knew what I had to do. He was gracious enough to accept to do the foreword for the book and also went ahead to give me some timeless pointers on the art of writing that enriched the work. Rev., I hope by this book your dream of inspiring the next generation of African writers has begun.

I also want to salute the contributions of the numerous individuals who have in diverse ways shaped my thoughts on the subject. To those who have ever attended any of my training programmes and seminars, I owe you a debt of gratitude. Your stories made me a better storyteller and your advice have made me a better coach. To those who make time every Monday to read my column in the *Business and Financial Times*, words cannot describe how much I appreciate you. Your encouragement and criticisms constantly put me on my toes. Finally, to all listeners of *Customers' World* on the Live Breakfast Club (www.livefmghana.com). This book is for you! You made it happen.

# FOREWORD

*By Rev. Albert Ocran*

*"It is not the employer who pays the wages. Employers only handle the money. It is the customer who pays the wages."*

—Henry Ford

Treating people well, delighting your customers and giving them moments to treasure should be the preoccupation of every service organization. Whether you run a bank, church, online business, farm, sporting club or services company, identifying your customers, anticipating their needs and meeting them faster, better or cheaper than the competition will ensure that you stay ahead of the pack.

Many notable organisations all over the world have risen to the top by applying this simple principle. A number of personal and organisational success stories can be traced to clearly identifying an existing or emerging customer need and meeting them innovatively.

Against this backdrop, this book "Customer Romance" by Jerry Halm is most timely and relevant. The author explores the correlation between romantic love and the relationship that should exist between service providers and their customers. He touches on important issues that must engage all sales and marketing executives, entrepreneurs, business leaders at all levels and literally anyone who deals with clients.

From the opening chapter on "The Business of Love" all the way through to what he calls "The Final Touch" the writer literally weaves his way through the various dynamics of customer service with dexterity and commitment. For someone who starts with a caveat that he is not an authority on love and romance, Jerry Halm shows through his work that he is a husband as well as a professional with two decades of experience in the area of sales and customer service. With this book, Jerry has joined the ever-growing legion of new African writers who are challenging the stronghold of ignorance with their God-given literary weapons.

One of the seminal lessons of this book is that customers overwhelmingly respond to great service with their wallets. This means that reading this book could also turn your financial fortunes and that of your organisation around. *Customer Romance* is an important addition to the body of knowledge on business leadership and I wholeheartedly recommend it to all.

*Albert Ocran,*
*Author, Minister and Management Consultant,*
*Accra-Ghana.*
*October 2013*

# A PROFESSOR'S PREVIEW

As a subject and a critical component of organisational strategy, *customer service* has grown in importance over the last few decades in both developed and developing economies. Deregulation in various industries, intense competition, variations in demand and the appropriation of emerging technologies are presenting daunting challenges to organisations, which globalisation is laying emphasis on.

Both manufacturing and services organisations as well as public and non-governmental institutions require innovative approaches in order to respond appropriately to these challenges. Additionally, the importance of effective customer service as a source of competitive edge has increased significantly over the last few decades.

During the same era, consultancy firms and business schools have been highlighting how fundamental it is for organisations to develop customer orientation. A cursory analysis would suggest that this message would seem to have hit home because today, many organisations profess to be customer oriented. Yet more often than not, organisations confuse promotion with customer orientation and the consequence is that in real marketing terms, they only succeed in producing a buzz phrase that is neither able to withstand the moment of truth nor test of time.

For marketing to truly have an effect on organisational performance, new skills must be deployed with the rightly associated new attitudes and behaviours. Clearly, the obstacles that impede the execution of well-grounded marketing practices may be ascribed to obsolete or incongruous organisational behaviour.

The attraction of this book lies in its ability to establish customer service as a significant component of market orientation and link the concept to overall organisational performance. This book highlights the overarching importance of customer service to organisational success regardless of the environment in which an organisation operates. Owing to the increasingly important role that customers play in the lives of organisations today and the fact that an organisation without loyal customers has no future, the issues emphasised in this book will remain relevant for generations to come. Indeed, I highly commend Jerry Halm for placing emphasis on the customer as central to the organisation.

Undoubtedly, every serious business student should be well acquainted with and have access to this book. For undergraduate and postgraduate courses in business, marketing and services management, the book would be a useful reading material. I also believe that lecturers, research scholars, and consultants would find it beneficial in having copies of this outstanding piece for reference in their libraries. Finally, for business executives, operating in today's competitive environment, this book is a must read for all who intend to remain relevant in their respective fields and subsequently take their organisations to new dimensions of success.

**Prof. Kwaku Appiah-Adu (Ph.D)**
Professor of Strategy & Marketing
Vice Dean, Central University Business School
Fellow, Centre for Advanced Strategic Analysis

# THE FIRST TOUCH

I will start with the sincerest of apologies. In the first place, I am not an authority on matters of love, romance or anything of that sort. If there is something that my brief experience in marriage has taught me, it is the fact that I know very little. My second reason for apologising is that I am also not, by any means, a doyen in matters of business. I see myself still clawing my way up the ladder of business success and recognition. I am yet to reach the top. In fact, I believe I have far less to teach than I have to learn.

So if I am not an expert in matters of romance or a master of business matters, what do I have to offer? I will tell you. What I am offering is a new way of looking at an old concept. I wrote this book to give a fresh impetus to the age-old crusade for better customer service all over the world.

I have been asked many times. Why *Romance*? My first answer? It's a beautiful word. Seriously though, the word describes that feeling of excitement that is associated with love. Or, as I like to put it, romance refers to the strong emotional ties that bind people in a relationship. In some ways, romance is synonymous with love.

After spending close to two decades in the area of sales and customer service—practising, managing, training, coaching, etc.—I have found out that many of the words and phrases many organisations use in describing their customers are so similar to the terms of endearment lovers have for each other. "Our cherished customers," "our lovely clients," "my wonderful customers" and "our lifelong partners" are just a few of those terms.

I have also found out that the actions involved in winning the heart of a loved one are akin to those of winning your share of a customer's pocket. The similarities between what a man (or woman) will do to win the love of another person and what an organisation will do to win a customer's business are so glaring. The result of studying these similarities is what you hold in your hands.

**CUSTOMER ROMANCE** is about creating love—not just any love, but love that rewards. It is a book for business owners, leaders, managers or professionals who want to become darlings to all their customers. It is for the individual (or business) that intends to bring some sunshine into the lives of customers. This is a book about how a business can win the hearts (and pockets) of its customers in a long-lasting relationship.

**CUSTOMER ROMANCE** is a staunch supporter of the relationship selling concept as against the transactional selling concept. This book advocates that no matter how much a business stands to lose in the short-run when it practises relationship building, in the long-run the relationship pays off. **CUSTOMER ROMANCE** debates that the most important ingredient in building a successful business is TRUST. However, trust is best established in a "romantic" relationship not in a mere transaction.

With that said, it is my great delight and singular honour to welcome you into the world of *CUSTOMER ROMANCE*!

# CHAPTER 1
## *THE BUSINESS OF LOVE*

*"A business that is not in love with its customers, but only the money they bring, should not expect love back."*

His heart was pounding as he raced behind the trees lining the street. He had to get to the junction in the next two minutes otherwise he was going to miss her. For weeks, he had been studying her movement. He knew the exact time she was going to close from lectures. This was the route she would normally use to get to her hostel and so it made sense to get to the junction at just the right time. He had to talk to her. It was now or never.

He just could not fathom what had gotten into him. The very first time his eyes met hers, he knew he was in love. She was something special. Her face was angelic, her gait regal and her mannerism, exquisite. He just could not get her out of his mind. He had been waiting for an opportunity to tell her his feelings. After weeks of dread and trepidation, he had finally mustered the courage and it must be today. As he neared the spot, a thousand thoughts ran through his mind. What was he really going to tell her? He had forgotten all the lines he had rehearsed over the past few days.

Just as he got to the last tree, he thought he heard someone call his name. He naturally turned to look. He was to regret that decision for a long time. He should not have. For with his back turned, he did not see the hawker who was coming from behind the same tree. They bumped into each other. He did not make much of the incident at first. He just apologised and turned to leave. That was when he realised the gravity of that simple incident.

An unusual wetness on his chest made him look down. He could not believe his eyes. The shirt was totally ruined. The woman had a bowl of palm nut oil in her hand which had spilled on his shirt. He had a decision to make. He could not see her like this. He had to go and change his shirt but that could mean losing her. What was he to do? He had to think fast. It is said that desperate times call for desperate measures and he was a desperate man. Without any second thought, he took off the shirt. He would rather face her in his vest than not face her at all. No sooner had he stripped down into his singlet than she emerged from the other side of the street. His heart missed a beat as he approached her. This was it. Now or never!

In the world of business, these are definitely desperate times. What does a business do in the face of tightening economic times, ever-fickle customers and overly-aggressive competitors? How does a business maintain a steady customer base that remains unwavering and religiously loyal in the face of more enticing offers from more "capable" adversaries?

After much thought into the best strategy a business can adopt to survive in these times, I realised the answer lies in an unusual direction—the world of romance. I see a strong semblance in what business leaders are going through in these times to what many people go through in attempting to ward off a competitor in a game of love.

I am convinced that most, if not all, of us will identify with a time when we had to use all means at our disposal to keep a *sweet love* from the powerful grips of another. I have been there and I believe you have been there also. How did you manage to win your love to your side and beat the competitor to it? How were you able to keep your lover's undying affection inspite of the fact that you might not have been the most "endowed" of the competitors? Within the answers to these questions lies the way forward for business leaders in these extremely competitive times.

It's great to be in love, so they say, and so have I experienced. The feeling is beyond description, especially if the love is as fresh as the morning dew. I am sure those who have ever been in love might be feeling nostalgic at this point in time. As I have already said, in thinking about the similarities between maintaining a romantic relationship and establishing a staunch customer base, I found so many instances of similitude.

Customer relationship is, in very many ways, akin to romantic relationships. Your lover (spouse, sweetheart, honey pie, or whatever "romantic" name you decide to call your better-half) is in every way your "customer." As Brian Tracy, the internationally-acclaimed motivational speaker, puts it, "the purpose of a business is to create and keep customers." What is the essence of a well-meaning romantic relationship if it is also not to create and keep a lover for life?

To state that *Customer Romance* is a new frontier will not be an absolute truism. This is because for decades, if not centuries, smart businesses have been wooing customers and providing them with good "romantic" experiences. However, as to it being a widely-recognised and widely-used business strategy, I daresay it would qualify as a novelty. Readers would agree, if they give much thought to it, that their feelings towards certain products and services they regularly patronise are nothing short of "love."

For every product that you are so in love with, there is almost always a better alternative. Even if there is no better alternative, product quality can always be replicated or even enhanced by a competitor. I very much doubt if this knowledge will make you change your favourite brand. What causes you to patronise that one particular product or service? It is the exceptional value you receive from using the product or service that keeps you going back to it. Come to think of it, isn't that what this whole business of love is about?

# CHAPTER 2
## *THE MASTERFUL LOVER*

*"He is not a lover who does not love forever."*

—Euripides, *Ancient Greek playwright*

He was, and still is, regarded as the first true ladies' man. Some call him "history's most famous lover." He was witty, charming and sly. Unfortunately, his name has become synonymous with love of the most sensual and playful kind. The preface to his memoirs reads *"I was born for the sex opposite to mine."* He was confidence personified, especially during his youthful days. This is what he says, *"My currency was an unbridled self-esteem."* He is none other than Giacomo Girolamo Casanova. He was one of those enigmatic historic figures whose fame grew substantially after their death than even while they lived.

Contrary to popular belief, Casanova was not the masterful lover modern scholars make him out to be. He had his faults as a human being and it was evident in the many struggles he faced. He was exiled twice from his home city of Venice, jailed for 15 months and suffered a number of venereal diseases due to his licentious lifestyle. He even admits that things were not too well with him as he aged. *"The power to please at first sight, which I had so long possessed in such measure, was beginning to fail me,"* he wrote.

It is therefore interesting that in spite of all the clear failings of Casanova as a wonderful lover, he is still held in such high regard as a great lover. He abused his charm over the opposite sex and still we write songs about him. About a third of his memoirs were used in describing various sexual partners he had during his gallivanting all over Europe, including encounters with maids, servants and prostitutes. Yet, we make movies about the man.

I have always wondered why there are some products and/or services that are not the very best in the market but customers still love them. In many of my training sessions, I ask participants what mobile telecommunications service provider they patronise. After hands have been raised, I ask which of the mobile telecom companies in the country they sincerely believe has the worst service. Most of the time, the answers are interesting: the same company that customers feel is offering the relatively worst service is the same company that majority of participants subscribe to. Why?

The answers vary. For some, they just do not want to go through the hustle of changing network service providers while for others, they do not see anything better being offered elsewhere. However an answer that always intrigues me when it pops up is when someone says, "I just like that company!" These individuals accept that the service is not the best it could be but they still stay with the brand.

I am of the opinion that the brands in question are masterful lovers. Like Casanova, these companies have succeeded in making all of their numerous customers fall so madly in love with them. Even though these customers are not too excited about the services of these organisations, they still stick to the brands-just like lovers sticking together in spite of some not-too-pleasant characteristics and actions of the significant other.

A masterful lover knows how to love. He knows the things he needs to do to make folks fall head over heels in love with him. Aside having knowledge of the fine art of loving, a masterful lover also knows his lover. He knows the likes and dislikes of his lover. He knows what will make the lover happy and what will make the lover sad. He has adequate knowledge about the very important things that concern his lover.

It is the same with the companies that have won the hearts of their cherished customers. I have realised that many corporate bodies throw the phrase "our cherished customers" about. How do you refer to someone as "cherished" if you know absolutely nothing about the person's likes and dislikes. A masterful lover derives no greater pleasure than in pleasing a woman, just as a romantic company derives no greater pleasure than in pleasing a customer.

What many companies fail to do is to place themselves as the lover of choice for their prospective suitors or partners, i.e. their customers. To be a masterful lover, you must learn to listen to your lover. Just as women love to be listened to, so do customers. Communication is key to winning the hearts of both your lover and your customer. I am told that a woman feels a whole lot better if she knows she has the full attention of her lover.

Customers are much like that—they love a company that treats them well and makes them feel special, as if they are the only customers the company has. Even if the business serves a million customers, it is important that every single customer is made to feel that the organisation exists only for him or her. Front-line staff must be well-trained enough to remember the names of as many customers as possible. Fortunately, there are numerous simple technological tools that are at the disposal of the modern business professionals to aid in the personalisation of services to each individual customer. Personalised service makes the customer feel special. That is just how a masterful lover makes his lover feels—very, very special.

# CHAPTER 3
## *IT IS ACTUALLY FEELINGS MANAGEMENT!*

*"The end result of a service experience is a feeling."*

(Karl Albrecht, *All That Matters*)

*Wal-Mart Customers **feeling** economic pressure-WSJ.com;*
*T-Mobile Leaves Customers **feeling** Left out with SGSII Variant –AndroidSPIN.com;*
*Oracle Customers **feeling** left out – informixmag.com;*
*BP Customers **feeling** Guilty?—dailymotion.com;*
*Auto repair shop leaves customers **feeling** dinged—miamiherald.com*

If an alien arriving on this planet for the first time came across these headlines, it would be forgiven if it concluded that customers were a breed of humans that only "felt." Such an assertion would not be too far from the truth. Customer service is all about FEELINGS! I am of the opinion that customer service is actually FEELINGS MANAGEMENT.

Feelings matter. As a matter of fact, sometimes feelings even matter more than facts. On the physical level, feelings keep us alive. Feelings aid us in differentiating between hot and cold, wet and dry, harmful and harmless, etc. Without feelings we would all be robots. Can you imagine not being able to feel anything? That would not only be scary but even life-threatening.

Beyond the physical, there is also the emotional aspect of feelings that we have to deal with. On a daily basis, we all experience a diverse range of emotions—some positive, others negative. From sadness to happiness, we all occasionally go through one emotion or the other. Not surprisingly, feelings or emotions have been found to play a very important role when it comes to business.

It is said that people buy for two main reasons—fear of loss or desire for gain. We are also told that of the two, the fear of loss is a more powerful emotion than the desire for gain. When it comes to customer service, feelings are so, so important.

A company that has great customer service is actually one that is very good at managing the feelings of its customers. Simple. Employees who excel in customer service are those that are better at managing (massaging!) the feelings of their customers. In other words, a customer service department is actually a department responsible for managing the feelings of customers.

The importance of feelings to customer service is made the more pronounced when one takes a look at the findings of a research study that sought to find out the reasons why customers stop doing business with a particular company. Let us analyse the findings for ourselves.

- 1% die
- 3% move
- 5% seek alternatives or develop other business relationships
- 9% begin doing business with the competition
- 14% switch due to product or service dissatisfaction
- 68% leave because they FEEL the sales person and company are

indifferent to their needs. They FEEL taken for granted. (Source: *U.S. Small Business Administration and the U.S. Chamber of Commerce.*)

The research findings above are evidence that it's all about feelings. More than two-thirds of your customers may stop doing business with you because of nothing more than their FEELINGS! I would have thought that the economic downturns and financial mishaps would make PRICE the greatest determinant in judging whether a customer would stay with a company or not. I am not alone in making this erroneous assumption. Take a look at a paper presented by the American Chamber of Commerce Executives and Corporate Research International on www.eyeonyourbusiness.com. According to the 2004 survey,

> *"74% of customers who stopped using a product or service cited customer service as a major factor in their decision. Research also revealed that business managers may be deceiving themselves about why customers leave. When asked, 49% of managers thought price was the primary reason their customers left. Only 22% cited customer service as the cause." (Source: The Customer Loyalty Solution.)*

The feelings of customers truly matter. A company that disregards the feelings of its customers will not be around for long. Interestingly, the evidence in some countries makes one wonder whether businesses are really aware of how their customers feel. Does the average business enterprise take time to understand the way its customers are feeling about the products and services it offers? I very much doubt that.

The irony of this is that you cannot use your *feelings* to gauge the feelings of your customers. You must do more than guesswork. I daresay that many companies find it so difficult to ask how their customers feel about what is being offered to them. A colleague tells me that maybe it is because these businesses are afraid of what their customers will say.

Organisations that refuse to regularly conduct simple customer satisfaction surveys are not really interested in knowing the feelings of their customers. I have been into customer service research long enough to know that a whole research can just be made up of one question. The shorter the research document, the greater the chances of your customers responding positively to it.

The whole research can be centred on a single question such as:

> How satisfied are you with doing business with us? or Are we meeting your needs?

Any one of these two simple questions, if handled well, will unearth the hidden feelings of a company's customers.

But what is a business to do after it gets to know the real feelings of its customers? I think it depends on the dominant feelings that are unearthed. If the survey reveals that customers feel great and positive about the company, then the task would be to maintain, or even improve on, the feelings of the customers. If, however, the feeling of a majority of customers is negative, then the job of the company would be to begin to cultivate some positive feelings. This would be akin to a man or woman attempting to rekindle love that has grown cold, which is no easy task.

Let us take a few minutes to look at some ways that businesses can adapt to keep the romance blossoming.

**Express your love in kind**

One sure way to get your customers to start feeling good about your company is to show the customers that you really care about them. Unexpressed love is no love at all, as far as I am concerned. You can easily express your love by regularly showing gratitude for the customer's loyalty. The company can occasionally organise Customer Appreciation Weeks just to let customers know that it truly cares about them.

However, on a more regular basis, customer-facing executives should, or indeed MUST, express their gratitude to customers. Regardless of the volume of business the customer does with the company, employees must always be appreciative of the customer for choosing that particular business and not the competition.

One easy way to make customers feel special at the individual level is to always refer to them by name. Referring to a person by name has a unique way of making people feel special. It tells customers that they are valued by the company. The customer would know that he or she is not just an unknown face in the crowd.

There are so many other ways a business can show a customer that it cares. The company can go the old-fashion way, by sending a *Thank You* card or even writing a formal letter of appreciation. To add some more class, you can even go ahead and frame the letter. This would make it easier for the customer to hang the framed letter somewhere prominent. It works magic with corporate customers.

The company can also go ahead with modernity and send a quick e-mail. This is very effective if it is done immediately after a purchase or immediately after the business relationship is established.

There is also the option of gifts. In many cultures, gift giving is usually a prelude to any form of courtship. It is reported that in rural Wales, guys would spend days on end handcrafting spoons that they would give to ladies of their choice. An acceptance of the spoon meant that courtship could proceed. Among the early English Puritans, it is claimed that the young ladies were given thimbles by their suitors in place of wedding rings. I could understand that choice of a gift since thimbles were needed for sewing—an important pastime at the time.

In some Nordic regions in the past, young ladies walked around with empty knife sheaths hanging around their waists. When a gentleman meets a lady he likes, he would place a knife in her sheath. If the lady keeps the knife, it means she has accepted the proposal; if she returns the knife, then she is not interested. The examples of gift-giving during courtship abound in many tribes and countries around the world.

Gift giving to loved ones is even practised at length in the animal kingdom, especially during mating or courtship. Many times, the gift would be a prey that has been hunted and killed by the male. There are times when the gifts given are not edible but they become objects to show off. We can learn a lot from birds, insects and other animals on the art of giving of gifts to win love. Sending gifts as a way of expressing gratitude and showing care is always in fashion. Gifts can range from cheap ones such as gift vouchers to very, very expensive ones such as houses and vehicles. It all depends on the financial will and capability of the company.

## Broadcast your love to the world

It is important to let the whole world know about love. I want to believe that this is one of the reasons why marriages are made public. It is an exhibition to the whole world that you have chosen this particular person out of all the seven billion inhabitants on planet Earth to spend your life with.

A cursory scan of the dailies reveals an increasingly-popular way by which companies are broadcasting their love to the world. It is becoming very popular for companies to take up full-page, full-colour advertisements in newspapers and magazines just to show that they are affiliated with particular individuals or corporate bodies. An individual wins an international accolade or even a local award and you can trust that there will be an advertisement by a company associating itself with that individual. A company is presented with an accolade and you see finance houses claiming ownership of the award-winning company's business.

A business can also broadcast the romance by placing testimonials about their cherished customers on its website. Broadcasting your relationship on the Net has business benefits for your customers. It creates a win-win situation for both parties. It provides free advertisement for the customer while at the same time endearing the business to that customer.

## Keep the flame burning

To make your customers feel special, it is important to ensure that you never make your customers feel left out. To go back to the study attributed to the *U.S. Small Business Administration and Chamber of*

Commerce, you will realise that 68% of customers leave because they feel taken for granted. One sure way to make loved ones feel taken for granted is to ignore them. This is why it is important that when it comes to customer service, the "Out of sight, out of mind" mantra should not be practised by any company.

Since it is proven that majority of customers will leave *without making noise* about their departure, companies should make conscious efforts at regularly linking up with their customers. One way to do so with some style is to remember customers on their birthdays, anniversaries and on public holidays. It keeps the flame of romance ever burning.

I daresay that the issue of customers' feelings is one that will hang around forever. Until businesses begin to value the feelings of their customers, we will continue to have customer service challenges in the business world. Maybe, as a first step in the recognition of this need, we can change the title of all Customer Service Departments to Feelings Management Departments. Are you feeling the new title?

# CHAPTER 4
## EMOTIONAL ILLITERACY

### A High Price to Pay

*My mother said I must always be intolerant of ignorance but understanding of illiteracy. That some people, unable to go to school, were more educated and more intelligent than college professors.*

(Maya Angelou)

*"It is turning out to be one of those days,"* Ama thought to herself as she settled behind her desk. She felt heavy within herself. She just could not place her finger on what was eating her up. All she knew was that, she had really not been herself that morning. She wished she had stayed at home but she had no choice. She was not just the client service executive at the publishing firm that she worked for; she was seen by many as the face of the company.

Ama loved her job. But this was one of those mornings when she wished she was somewhere else. She was yet to receive her first customer for the day but already she had started experiencing a slight headache. Admittedly, the headache had started this morning even before she left the house. Ama was well aware of the implications of that slight lingering headache around that time of the month.

With the air-conditioning unit also malfunctioning the day before, she knew she was in for a hard time. She could not stand the heat and she had made her boss aware of that. However, nothing had still been done and she was not happy about that. Frankly, handling customers was not something she was really looking forward to that morning. She was brooding over her predicament with her head bowed when the doors of the reception opened and in walked her first customer. "Here we go," Ama muttered to herself.

As the customer approached her desk, she noticed that he was not smiling. Ama could not be bothered. She was also having a bad day, so why bother with a customer's bad mood? What Ama had not realised was that the customer's frown was in response to the frown he had seen on her face as he entered. Ama was unaware that her internal mood was being exhibited openly on her face. Her body language was also accentuating that negative ambience around her. The customer was just reflecting Ama's mood.

The danger was that Ama's negative mood had the potential of generating a downward spiral that could affect her whole day, making an already bad day, worse. But she was oblivious to this fact. All she cared about was that she was in a bad mood and wanted to get out of the office. Physically she was in the office but mentally, she was somewhere else.

Down the hall from Ama's office, Adjoa was also bemoaning her bad luck that morning. She had accidentally stained her white blouse that morning while having breakfast with her colleagues. That seemingly little incident had so dampened her spirit that even though she had managed to wipe the oily stain off, she was still "not herself."

What had worsened the situation for Adjoa was a remark by one of her colleagues to the effect that only uncouth women stained their attire when eating. Although the comment had been made in a spirit of conviviality, Adjoa was not too pleased with it. She felt her colleague had gone too far with that joke.

Just as she settled behind her desk to prepare for the day's work, her supervisor stormed into the reception. He was displeased with the fact that Adjoa had not been at her desk at exactly 8 o'clock when the first customers would usually have walked in. Thankfully, no customer had appeared by the time of this tirade. Adjoa tried to explain the situation with the stained blouse but her boss was having none of that.

Adjoa had her head bowed throughout her supervisor's ranting. Obviously, her day was not getting any better. But something dramatic was to happen. As Adjoa's supervisor stormed away from the reception, the doors to the reception swung open. Adjoa lifted her head up and, as if by some magical transformation, her face was instantly lit up.

In the twinkle of an eye, she had managed to transform herself from the lady in pain to a smiling, cheerful front desk executive. She was instantly beaming with smiles and brimming with confidence as she welcomed her first customer for the day. Adjoa's ability to effectively manage her moods and emotions was the key to her amazing success at the front desk of her company. She was really good at her job!

Experts will describe Ama and Adjoa differently in terms of how they went about handling their emotions. Adjoa would be described as being emotionally-literate with Ama being described as an emotional illiterate.

The issue of emotional literacy (or illiteracy) is gradually assuming great importance in the corporate world. This is because business managers and leaders are looking for that additional "ingredient" that can make their staff perform to their utmost best. It has been realised that their CVs are not giving a good indication of the prospective employee's ability to manage their emotions. Candidates with good grades and perfect CVs have been employed but who have performed abysmally. There is a missing ingredient and gradually we are being told the secret might lie with our emotions.

The term emotional literacy has been defined by Professor Katherine **Weare** of the University of Southampton as

> *"the ability to understand ourselves and other people; and in particular to be aware of, understand and use information about emotional states of ourselves and others with skill and competence. It includes the ability to understand, express and manage our own emotions and respond to the emotions of others in ways that are helpful to ourselves and others."*

An amusing definition of the term is given by Steve Hein of *eqi.org*. He defines Emotional Literacy as

*the ability to express feelings with specific feeling words, in 3 word sentences.*

In other words, an emotionally literate individual is one who recognises and makes the right use of his or her emotions. An emotionally literate person is one who has that ability to identify his or her feelings specifically.

*"I don't want to be at the mercy of my emotions. I want to use them, to enjoy them, and to dominate them."* (Oscar Wilde, Irish writer and poet)

To be emotionally-intelligent is to know specifically how one is feeling in a given situation. Experts aver that the more specific we are about the particular emotion, the better we are at managing it. Ama knew she was not in a good mood but she did not specifically identify what was eating her up.

Emotional literacy allows an individual to know how to handle emotionally-charged situations without losing his or her cool. Emotional literacy enables the individual to, not only control his emotions but also to control the effects of the emotions of others. As humans, emotions play a very important role in our day-to-day interactions.

> *"People will forget what you said, people will forget what you do, but people will never forget how you made them feel."* (Jason Barger, American Author, Speaker, and Consultant)

The emotions we generate in our customers are of great importance as they will linger for a long time. If the essence of customer service is to ensure that the customer keeps coming back, then it is of utmost importance that the customer always walks away with the right emotions.

Great customer service executives are those that are literate in reading their own emotions. They have the ability to manage their most distressing emotions. Adjoa showed that ability in the way she handled the situation that morning. Emotions affect our thoughts and therefore our actions. If Adjoa had not taken a hold of her distressing emotions, she might have made a mess of herself that morning.

Primarily, our emotions are of two main types: those that generate comfort and those that generate discomfort. Customers come to do business with you because they have a belief and an expectation that doing business with you, and not the competition, will lead to greater comfort. We must therefore manage our emotions to ensure that we make customers feel that being with us drives them towards a state of comfort.

The number of enquiries I received after an article I once wrote on *Emotional Intelligence* indicates that interest in this subject is growing. Some readers wanted to know how they could become emotionally literate. I must state that I am no expert in the field. I am just a curious brain always seeking for ways to ensure that customer service excellence becomes a reality all over the world. However, there are a number of experts on the Internet offering online courses on Emotional Literacy. I do not recommend or advocate any particular one since I am yet to personally take any of such courses.

The closest I will come to any form of recommendation will be to ask readers to take a look at Mark Zimmerman's website *emotionaliteracyeducation.com*. It is one of those few sites that provide in-depth insight into the subject of Emotional Literacy. Zimmerman even discusses what he refers to as the "vocabulary" and "language of emotional literacy." I am pretty sure you will find some useful information on this site.

Besides that, however, I want to believe that all it takes to begin a mastery of your emotions is to give the subject some thought. It pays to give some thought to your emotions before you do anything. Acquiring some education on the subject is good but I feel we can start on our own to learn how to read our own moods and emotions. After all, if there is one person that has been with you all your life and would be an automatic authority on the subject of YOU it would be YOU! Yes, you yourself! Who knows YOU more than YOU?

I very much doubt if Adjoa had acquired some education on the subject of Emotional Literacy but she displayed exceptional emotional literacy skills when it mattered most. The story with Ama was a bit different. She was not a bad worker. The issue was that she was a stark illiterate when it came to the matter of her emotions. Her inability to read and make meaning of her emotions affected her performance. This is a challenge many of us face on a daily basis. We might be well-read on many subjects but illiterates when it comes to reading our emotions. It is time we begin to take emotional literacy seriously because If we fail to do so, we might end up paying a high price.

# CHAPTER 5
## *LOVING FROM INSIDE OUT*

**Internal Customer Romance Pays**

*"I have an everyday religion that works for me. Love yourself first, and everything else falls into line."*

—Lucile Ball, 1911-1989,
American Comedienne and Actress

The hall had been so well-decorated. The rows of ribbons had been carefully matched with the rows of balloons and flowers. The atmosphere was solemn but yet there was an anxiety in the air. The guests were already seated. A tuxedoed gentleman behind the grand piano was serenading the gathering. He filled the room with smooth melodies that added to the blissful mood in the hall. As the tune he was playing came to an end, a door by the side of the stage opened. A man in a dark suit walked in and took his place in the middle of the stage, fully facing the congregation. It was time.

Suddenly, there was a buzz of activity around the huge doors that served as the main entrance into the hall. Ushers took their positions just as the *Wedding March* boomed from the grand piano. The doors opened slowly and wide. For a second, those inside had to squint to get a good look at her as she gracefully walked in. She was resplendent in her long, peacock-blue satin wedding gown with a bouquet of white roses in her hand. Slowly, she inched her way up the stage to where the presiding minister in the dark suit stood.

Everything seemed so well-timed and so well-rehearsed. For some, it looked any other wedding. And in many ways, it was. But this was no ordinary wedding. This was historic. It was a wedding that would discard the age-old concept of "the two becoming one." This was because she was getting married to the one person she loved more than any other person on earth. Herself!

As a budding author, the titles of books have always fascinated me. I am of the opinion that titles call out to you. We do not buy books but rather books choose us. After you have been chosen by a specific book, it is the title that actually does the calling—or shouting out. Recently as I traversed the wondrous expanse of the Internet, I chanced on a book with quite an interesting title. The book, written by Dr. Cherie Carter-Scott, is titled "If Love Is a Game, These Are the Rules" and it immediately caught my attention. I am yet to get a copy but I had the chance to read excerpts of it and I think it will make for interesting reading.

Of the many "rules" that she wrote about, there is one that I feel is worth sharing. This particular rule rests on the fact that it would be very difficult to establish a good relationship with any other person if you first and foremost do not love yourself. Instructively, this happens to be her Rule Number One. Specifically, this is how she puts it:

*"Your relationship with yourself is the central template from which all others are formed. Loving yourself is a prerequisite to creating a successful and authentic union with another."*

I am aware that this way of thinking might not go down well with the beliefs of some. To some people, it might be selfish to love yourself first. I will beg to differ if you hold such a view. As one writer has said, "*It is not selfish to love yourself first—it is self-responsible.*" According to the writer, those who attend to their own feelings and needs so that they are not demanding and needy of others are actually self-responsible.

*"To love others, we must first learn to love ourselves." – Anonymous*

However, I want to believe that those calling for self-loving are actually not advocating some of the weird things people are doing these days—with particular reference to the phenomenon of Me-Weddings. That is a bit over the board, if you ask me. In my opinion, getting married or wedded to your own self does not qualify as self-loving. If after waiting for years, a Mr Right does not show up, getting married to yourself is not the best option. Exchanging vows with your inner self and exchanging rings with your "inner groom" is far from being empowered.

Every business has internal and external customers. Although much of the "romance" we have spoken about is directed at external customers, there should be both external and internal customer romance. The concept of an internal customer is something that one cannot do away with when it comes to customer service. Any employee who receives goods or services produced elsewhere in the organisation as inputs to his or her work must be regarded as a customer.

Just like external customers, internal customers also have needs that have to be met. Just as any encounter between an external customer and a customer-facing executive counts as a Moment of Truth, so does any encounter between two employees in the same firm.

On a daily basis, there are numerous service encounters occurring between colleagues in the office which have tremendous effects on the overall service quality of the organisation. If there is to be a great "romance" between a business and its external customers, there must first be internal customer romance. A business must first love itself, i.e. its employees, before it would have any chance of building a great relationship with its external customers.

A study first published in the *International Journal of Service Industry Management* in 1994 by three researchers (Gremler, Bitner and Evans) set out to find out whether the same events and behaviours associated with service satisfaction or dissatisfaction for external customers apply also to internal customers. In other words, do internal customers look out for the same things in their interactions with internal service providers?

Using the critical incident technique, the researchers gathered stories from employees of a large American bank. The stories were actually incidents that the individual or someone they knew had either handled well or poorly. The stories were then critiqued in order to understand the events and behaviours associated with each incident. To ensure a good balance, the researchers selected employees from each department and geographic area of the bank. The respondents sampled were asked to provide descriptions of two stories (i.e. internal service encounter experiences). One story was expected to be of a good (or favourable) experience and the other of a bad (unfavourable) experience.

According to the researchers, they received a total of 251 stories or critical incidents. However, they were only able to use 183 of the narrations which they subjected to further analysis. To do a good analysis, the researchers fell on an earlier study. In a 1990 study published in the Journal of Marketing, a group of researchers used the same critical incident technique to study the way external customers differentiate between satisfactory and unsatisfactory experiences. Using 700 incidents narrated by these external customers, the researchers of this earlier study were able to identify particular events and related behaviours of contact employees that caused the external customers to differentiate very satisfactory services from very dissatisfactory ones.

Three kinds of behaviours were identified. These were operationalized as **Recovery** – employee response to service delivery system failures; **Adaptability** – employee response to customer needs and requests; and **Spontaneity** – unprompted and unsolicited employee actions.

Recovery as a behaviour was linked to the following events: unavailable service, unreasonably slow service, company errors and other core service failures. Adaptability as a behaviour was linked to the following incidents: customers with "special needs," customer preferences, admitted customer error and potentially disruptive others. Spontaneity was linked with the following events: Attention paid to customer, truly out-of-the-ordinary employee behaviour, employee behaviours in the context of cultural norms, Gestalt evaluation and performance under adverse circumstances.

To determine if there were any similarities between internal and external customers, the 1994 study of the American bank decided to use the same methodology used by the researchers in the 1990 study. There are some more technicalities with the study that I would not want to bother readers with. The long and short of the story is this: "Internal customers are similar to external customers in that the same general events and behaviours of service providers are associated with satisfaction or dissatisfaction in both types of service encounters."

For someone like me, the findings are quite revealing. All too often, we tend to concentrate our efforts on satisfying the external customer and totally neglect the internal customer. Whenever we say the "customer is always right," it is the external customer that comes to mind. If the results of this study are anything to go by, then we need a re-think. We need to look for ways to ensure that every single staff gets to really appreciate the Internal Customer Service concept. Staff must be made to understand that they are serving customers, and not just dealing with colleagues. This is the only way to build that strong service-oriented culture Gremler, Bitner and Evans wrote about.

Management must make conscious efforts to put structures in place to create a culture where the responses to the needs of the internal customer are as prompt, empathetic and reliable as the responses to the needs of the external customer. The same effort that is put into ensuring that the tangibles of the service experience are always kept right for the external customers must also be put into those for the internal customer. This also means that customer service managers, leaders and supervisors must endeavour to constantly monitor the satisfaction levels of internal customers to ensure that dissatisfaction is either non-existent or kept at the very minimum.

There is one other suggestion from the research under discussion which I believe is of some importance. The researchers stated that "one way to increase the satisfaction of internal customers is to give employees the freedom to grant special requests made by fellow employees." Internal service providers such as the IT department must have the freedom to handle other employees who might not be so adept at this ICT thing. ICT staff, in dealing with other staff, must be very supportive and not dismissive, as is the case most of the time.

I am sure the discussion on these findings can go on and on in our various offices. But the point here, I believe, has been well stated. We need to remember that what is good for the goose is also good for the gander. For profit sake, we must go out of our way and "romance" our external customers but we must not do so to the detriment of the feelings of those inside. If you must love, then you must from the inside out. As the Irish poet Oscar Wilde once said: *"To love oneself is the beginning of a life-long romance."*

# CHAPTER 6
## *A CASE FOR THE HUMAN TOUCH*

*"Nothing eases suffering like human touch."*

Bob Fischer, *American author*

The research was to test the power of the human touch. A box was placed in a public telephone booth and money intentionally left in the box. People who came into the booth to make calls would normally check inside the box to see if someone might have dropped some pocket change in there. Many people normally take any money they find away. For the experiment, however, as soon as the individual is done with the call and steps out of the booth, he or she is approached by one of those involved in the study and asked if they had found any money in the box. It was reported that 97% of those approached claimed that they did not find any money in it. In other words, they lied.

It was however interesting to note that the same study was carried out again but this time with a slight difference. When the caller is approached, the researcher will stretch out and touch the person. Believe it or not, the statistics changed. This time 95% of those approached claimed that they had found money in the box. They even went ahead and handed the money over to the one who approached them. Amazing! Just by touching, the *humanness* in people showed up.

The power of the human touch is something we cannot treat lightly. There are a number of studies that attest to the ability of touch to do wonders in our lives. The human touch has been found to enhance the growth of children. Children who were brought up in homes where the positive, loving human touch was prevalent turned up to be more responsible adults. There are even studies that prove that touching can prevent some common ailments.

In a quest to keep abreast with the times, many businesses are engaged in an Information and Communications Technology race with competitors. Anyone who has experienced the advantages provided by new software and state-of-the-art gizmos, gadgets and widgets will know that they are good and very much a necessity in these times.

Managing a large customer base is a task that can pose a major challenge to even well-resourced organisations. Therefore, the proliferation of advanced information and communications technology is a welcome relief to most firms and money spent to beef up an organisation's technological backbone is money well spent. In this day and age, technology is a key element in ensuring a company's success. Through technological enhancements, operations of many companies have been greatly improved, ultimately benefiting not only the companies but their customers too.

However, no number of ICT tools and software can do everything by themselves. There is something that should be added to the new technology to give a totally exhilarating customer experience: the human touch. If, as a business, you have the sole right to use a certain technology and all your competitors have been banned from using that technology or anything like it, then you can stop reading at this point. Fortunately or unfortunately, this is not so. No one business can boast of being the sole repository of all technological know-how.

> *"You'll never have a product or price advantage again. They can be easily duplicated, but a strong customer service culture can't be copied."*

> —*Jerry Fritz, Acclaimed Customer Service Trainer*

Whatever software or technology a business invents or adopts can be replicated by the competition. *Romantic* organisations know that it is not enough to compete on price or technology advantages alone. This is because there always seems to be a competitor who possesses better technology or can do things cheaper. There are no guarantees in this competitive environment. However, one of the best guarantees that can ensure customer retention is to provide superior customer service.

Provision of superior customer care distinguishes smart firms from their average competitors. The quality of human relations between smart businesses and their customers is exceptional. These companies emphasise the human touch as opposed to the tech-touch. They know that customers find it difficult, if not impossible, to fall in love with a machine. People want to connect to other people, not machines.

> *"People don't want to communicate with an organization or a computer. They want to talk to a real, live, responsive, responsible person who will listen and help them get satisfaction."*

> —*Theo Michelson, State Farm Insurance, USA*

Customers shop not only for material goods but also to have an experience. Starbucks is a good example of a company that has tapped into this expectation. The international coffee chain has created a warm, friendly environment that makes customers "feel good." Successful hotels, restaurants, and other service businesses understand that one essential way of distinguishing themselves from their competitors is by providing high-quality service with a distinctive human touch. This is the customer romance approach. These businesses know that no matter how advanced robots get, they will never match up to good old human beings.

Can you imagine an ATM striving to create rapport, communication, trust, and credibility with a client? Have you come across a smiling ATM? If you have, call me. These technologically-advanced means of serving customers are extremely important but my point is that they cannot replace the human touch. It is the human touch that maintains the long-lasting customer romance. Eye-to-eye contact is important in handling customers. Romantic companies do not let automation get between the front-line employee and the customer.

To buttress my point, I will quote from the bestseller "*In Search of Excellence: Lessons from America's Best-Run Companies*". In a chapter captioned 'Close to the Customer', it states:

> "Being customer-oriented doesn't mean that our excellent companies are slouches when it comes to technological or cost performance. But they do seem to us more driven by their direct orientation to their customers than by technology or by a desire to be the low-cost producer. Take IBM, for example. It is hardly far behind the times, but most observers will agree that it hasn't been a technology leader for decades. Its dominance rests on its commitment to service."

The IBM example is particularly intriguing because, in my opinion, IBM is a global technological giant. If IBM is said to be dominant because of its commitment to service, then what should smaller players concentrate on? IBM has been described by some as being *"market—and customer-driven, not technology-driven."* In other words, excellent businesses adopt good technology to boost their operations and delivery but their main interest is in establishing and maintaining a good relationship with their customers.

Companies that tend to focus solely on technology without enhancing the human touch are playing a risky game. It is the same as the man (or woman) who builds a whole relationship on just material things. The material things have a vital role to play in the relationship but what if someone else with more wealth comes along? You will end up losing the love of that 'customer.'

Sometime ago, a leading financial house with branches across many African countries switched software to stay abreast of the times and this bank faced serious trouble. The switch-over did not go too well. The bank, which was a model of efficiency and excellent customer service, now had to contend with frequent shutdowns of the system, long queues of impatient customers and a gradual deterioration of an otherwise well-polished image.

I was in one of its branches and I witnessed first-hand how quickly customers could easily lose their "love" for a brand. However, I believe the bank was able to weather the storm mainly due to the human touch of its staff, especially some tellers. Can you imagine what would have happened if this bank had built all of its success around its technological superiority? Customers would have simply switched their loyalty to the next technology leader in the market.

# CHAPTER 7
## *TOUCHING CUSTOMERS AT THE RIGHT PLACES*

**Feeling your Way to the Heart**

*"Touch has a memory."*

John Keats, *English Romantic poet*

The word '*touch*' is a touchy subject—so much so that one dictionary lists sixty (60) separate meanings for the word. There is so much to learn about the science and art of touch. Those who claim to be 'experts' in the study of human interactions and communications know that one of the most important aspects of maintaining a great relationship is in how one uses the power of touch. Knowing when to touch someone, when not to even dare and how to touch the one will go a long way to help you create a satisfying relationship. We all know that one wrong touch can earn one a very dirty slap or even a trip to the nearest Police Station.

As it is in human relations, so is it with business relations. Businesses also touch their patrons, prospects or customers in more ways than one. Regardless of whether the business people are aware of it or not, the business is constantly touching those who come into contact with it. This is where **Customer Touchpoints** come in.

Customer touchpoints are defined as all of the physical, communication and human interactions that customers experience during their relationship with a business. One writer defines the term as:

> *"Every point of contact between a business and its customers—online and off. Each communication, human resource, branding, marketing and sales process initiative creates touchpoints. The quality of touchpoint experiences drives perceptions, actions and relationships."*

Others have defined customer touchpoints as "channels of communication with which businesses interact directly with their customers."

Another writer defines touchpoints as *"customer interaction channels such as call centres, web sites, automated teller machines and web kiosks."* No matter the definition one prefers, it is obvious that customer touchpoints are essential in winning and keeping customers for life.

The last definition I came across claims that touchpoints refer to *"every point in time the business connects with its customers throughout the entire product/service delivery; pre-, during and post-purchase."*

The last definition breaks down touchpoints into three categories—those the customer experiences before purchase, those the customer experiences during the actual exchange and those connections the customer experiences after the purchase.

These categories therefore will include office buildings, print, electronic and "verbal" advertisements, brochures, fliers, letter heads, websites and email addresses, sales and customer service professionals, invoices, corporate uniforms and attire, company-branded vehicles, etc. All these form touchpoints through which customers experience the business but it must be said that the product or service is the main touchpoint. However, concentrating on the product or service without paying much attention to these other touchpoints will spell doom for the brand.

If you are still not sold on the importance of managing your business' touchpoints, I would like you to consider the fact that customers form perceptions of your business and brand based on their cumulative touchpoint experiences. Every single moment that a customer encounters your brand through a touchpoint, there is an opportunity to create and reinforce a positive impression. Based on the impressions made through the touchpoints, the customer can decide to come back or to stay away.

Smart businesses know how to take advantage of all possible customer touchpoints. They do not take anything for granted. They are aware that there are some touchpoints that could easily be overlooked and as such pay particular attention to them. Just as with human relations and interactions, there are "hard" and "soft" touches or touchpoints. I tend to define the "soft touch" as those points of contact whose impression remain mainly at the subconscious level. The "hard touch" will refer to those contact points that you relate to at the conscious level. You are consciously aware of those points of interaction.

Customers rarely go out of their way to pay attention to these "soft" contacts points but if there is an issue with them, customers notice it. A customer who enters a business' premises will not be too concerned about something as mundane as a doormat but if there is a dirty bedraggled doormat, the customer will notice it. This seemingly insignificant matter can have a lasting impression on the customer.

A customer who walks into a supermarket to shop has one thing on his or her mind—to buy whatever he or she needs, or to window-shop, in some cases. However, if the sales attendant has one button missing on her uniform or an oil stain on her dress, chances are that the customer will notice it. This "little" matter could affect the chances of the customer coming back to shop at that particular supermarket. That is the power of "soft" touchpoints.

I hope by now I have managed to convince you to take a second look at all the ways you are touching your customers. I hope you have resolved to take steps to better manage your customer touchpoints. In these times, managing your customer touchpoints is not optional; it is a must. If you intend to embark on Customer Touchpoints Management, I believe the following ideas will be of great help.

## CTM-Customer Touchpoint Management

### 1. Identify customer touchpoints

There is a general agreement among experts in the field that the first thing to do in CTM is to list down all the possible customer touchpoints that your organisation has. One way to go about this is to audit all the processes your customers go through to access whatever service or product you are offering. Take a walk through your business processes. Every single step in the process will contain a number of touchpoints and the goal of the business is to make sure that each touchpoint will create and reinforce all the positive attributes of the brand. The end process of this exercise will be a detailed touchpoint map of your organisation.

## 2. Touchpoint Categorization

This is another important step in Customer Touchpoint Management. Depending on the kind of business an organisation is engaged in, some touchpoints will play a far more important role in determining the impressions that customers have of the business than others. As one writer puts it, "All touchpoints are not created equal." For instance, under normal circumstances the aroma in a restaurant will be of far greater importance than that in an auto mechanic's shop. Can you imagine entering a restaurant that smelled like an auto mechanic's shop? As far as I am concerned, the surest way to categorise your touchpoints is to ask your customers what is important to them.

## 3. The Ideal Touchpoints

After you have a very good idea of the kind of touchpoints you have and the importance customers attach to them, you must design the ideal touchpoints. These touchpoints must be in alignment with your corporate vision and mission—your raison d'être. Consistency is the key to ensuring that touchpoints work for you.

Businesses that have more touchpoints have a greater chance of engaging their customers than those with fewer touchpoints. However, the more touchpoints a business tends to have, the greater the challenge of maintaining consistency. The challenge therefore is for businesses to create more touchpoints with customers while at the same time strengthening those connections on a regular basis.

Whether you accept it or not, there is some "touching" going on between your organisation and its prospects and customers. Are your customer touchpoints "touching" customers in the right way? Are you touching customers in a way that gives them a "good feeling"? Is your touch having the right effect on your cherished customers? Are your invoices accurate? Is your office space portraying the kind of image that will make people take you serious? Are your ads creating the right impressions? Is your website design a positive reinforcement of your corporate image? These are some of questions that you have to answer on a daily basis if you intend to stay in business for long.

Great companies know that customer relationships in these times call for more than just having a great product (or service) backed by a great sales team. Customers have to be wooed until they fall so deeply in love with your offering that they will ward off advances from potential suitors. No matter how well you perform as a business, there are little things that can cause the relationship with your customers to suffer. The companies, products and/or services that we love are those that "touch" us in the right places at the right times. After all, that is what *"romancing"* the customer is all about—feeing your way to the customer's heart.

# CHAPTER 8
## *RICH DIALOGUE: RICHER EXPERIENCES*

### The Foundation to a Great Romance

*One plus one makes two but two monologues do not make a dialogue.*

Today's customer is a totally different animal. Today's customer is so immersed in the deluge of promotional messages that he has become virtually oblivious to any attempts to get his attention. Like a drowning man, today's customer makes every attempt to escape from the deluge. A 2010 research carried out on behalf of Deloitte indicated that 86% of people will normally skip a TV ad. An earlier survey conducted by Opinion Matters for HowTo.tv in 2007 had also intimated that *"84% of 25-34 year-olds have left a favourite website because of intrusive or irrelevant advertising . . . . 44% of direct mail is never opened."* Like one writer said, today's customers are "overstimulated."

Today's customer is also Internet-savvy. She knows how to get any information she wants by just a click of a button. She is aware that the competitor's contact details are just a touch away. She uses the Internet to gather information about the business and its products. Today's customer will not hesitate to use social media platforms to speak his mind on an unpleasant experience. Competition has handed the staff of authority over to the customer. Today's customer knows this and cannot be convinced otherwise. Today's customer believes she has "earned" the right to speak her mind and, given the opportunity, she will.

Today's customer is re-shaping the business landscape. Today's customer is concerned about things that did not matter some years ago. She wants to know what values the organisation stands for. She wants to know about the organisation's stance on child labour, famine, drought, and other socio-economic issues. She even wants to know what the business is doing about global warming. So you see, dealing with today's customer is a totally different ballgame.

However, of all the traits, characteristics, attributes and habits of today's customers, the one that has serious consequences for businesses is this-today's customer does not want to be just spoken to. She wants to be engaged in a dialogue. Today's consumer expects to be part of the conversation about the product and/or service on offer. Today's customer does not want to be fed with advertisements. Collaboration is what excites today's customer.

Businesses must accept that today's customer does not want to be told what to do. She wants to be asked what is to be done. Today's customer will resent any attempts to stifle her voice. She will switch to the competition in protest against any such attempts. It is for this reason that customer communications must be converted from a one-way monologue model to a two-way dialogue or conversation model.

Conversation fertilizes our understanding and that is why customers are demanding that businesses converse with them rather than talk down to them. The benefits of having sustained conversations with customers are enormous. Among other benefits, an open, honest dialogue builds trust with customers. Businesses that give customers a listening ear are viewed as being more trustworthy by customers. Customers tend to view those companies that encourage dialogue as being more transparent than those that shy away from engaging with their customers.

Open communications has been, and will always be, the bedrock for any solid relationship, including that between a business and its customers. I am sure you will be much more comfortable dealing with a business whose CEO you can directly call than one that will have you go through several hurdles to get someone high up to talk to. What do you think will happen if you were to walk into a shop and found two competing products, one product with a toll-free number while the other had no such information on? I am sure you will be more comfortable going for the one that provides you with an avenue for a conversation.

Dialogue also makes customers feel important. We all love it when our views are considered. When customers know that their views are cherished, they go the extra mile to ensure that they make their views known. When customers know that their views have been heard and actions taken on those views, they begin to feel a sense of ownership of the business. A sense of ownership comes with attendant loyalty for the brand.

Closer connection and conversations with customers has several other benefits for the business organisation. Stories of very profitable products and services being developed with the help of customers are widespread. Companies have used their constant dialogue with customers to come out with products that have become big hits. Bill Gates was reported to have stated that about 80% of product improvements of Microsoft were based on feedback from their customers. By engaging in open, honest and timely conversations with customers, it is possible to pick up changing customer preferences and tastes way before your competitors.

Aside these, there is another reason why dialoguing with one's customers is crucial. The correlation between brand loyalty and richer business-customer dialogue is well documented. In his book, *REAL TIME: Preparing for the Age of the Never Satisfied Customer*, Regis McKenna writes:

> *"How in this environment can companies create and maintain brand loyalty? The answer is to alter brand definition so as to supply what has been missing from the picture: **a rich dialogue** between producers and consumers . . ."*

Organisations that intend to become the darlings of customers must go beyond just giving customers the opportunity to voice out opinions about their experiences with the brand. They must go beyond responding to customer issues, opinions and complaints with the "business as usual" attitude. Customer-centric companies or the businesses that win the hearts and pockets of customers are those that ensure that there are systems in place which enable customers to receive responses in real time. How would you feel if you were conversing with someone who took a long time to respond? That would definitely not be a rich dialogue, if you ask me.

Businesses must engage their customers in rich dialogue. That is the way to ensure richer customer experiences and we live in an age where the opportunities for engaging customers are everywhere. Advancement in ICT has placed various platforms, tools and applications at the disposal of organisations to enable a closer connection with their patrons and customers. The website has ceased to be just an addition or an afterthought to a business's infrastructure. It is a must.

There is so much opportunity for businesses to engage with customers using their websites. For instance, businesses can set up blogs on their site for customers to post reactions and opinions on issues that concern them. Companies can even add chatrooms to their sites to enable continuous dialogue with their customers.

I am sure there are some other ways that organisations can use to engage their customers in a continuous dialogue that would result in a win-win situation. It is becoming increasingly common to see businesses take to Social Media platforms to engage with their customers. I personally think that is a smart move. Your customers are virtually living their lives on the Internet, so what is wrong with joining them there? If we will travel all the way to engage customers in their areas of abode and business locations, what prevents us from meeting them on Facebook or Google+?

Interestingly, I have noticed that the quest to engage in rich dialogue with customers transcends service providers to even product manufacturers. It is now a common practice to see products such as canned food with toll-free numbers, email address and website. I have on my desk a tin of Nestle's *Ideal Milk* and it has an inscription captioned **Good to talk** which comes with the website and a phone number of the company. This information is on all the products of Nestle that I have in my locker.

That is an opportunity for dialogue created by Nestle and I respect them for the attempt. I am mentioning this because there are other products in that same locker and some do not have an address, let alone a website address. The PG TIPS teabag in the locker also comes with additional information such as toll-free number, which even indicates the exact time to call between Mondays and Fridays.

It is a fact that we have come to a juncture where businesses must accept that the future will be built around a more collaborative approach with customers. The barriers that used to exist between organisations and businesses are coming down faster than the Berlin Wall did. Customers of today and, I daresay, the future will become increasingly more demanding of that sort of collaboration. Customers will demand improved conversations with service providers and product manufacturers.

Like sharks that have smelled blood, today and tomorrow's customers will ferociously demand more—more considerations, more respect and more dialogue. Smart business owners, leaders, managers and CEOs are aware of this and are preparing themselves for it. In a document titled *"Capitalizing on Complexity: Insights from the Global Chief Executive Officers Study"* prepared by the IBM Institute for Business Value in May 2010, it was revealed that 88% of CEOs interviewed intimated that "getting closer to customers" was the top priority for their businesses over the next five years.

Customers expect richer experiences when they come into contact with our brands and richer experiences come from having rich dialogue. Businesses that refuse to become more open to rich dialogues with their customers will be punished badly. Businesses that are keen on only feeding customers with information without opening channels for customer feedback will soon find themselves left behind. Survival in these times calls for rich dialogue for richer experiences.

# CHAPTER 9
## *CUSTOMER INTIMACY*

### The Closer, the Better

*"The more you get to know a person, the more attractive they become to you."*

Unknown

*Intimate (adj.)*: Marked by close acquaintance, association or familiarity.
*Synonyms*: affectionate, dearest, loving, fond, close, warm, etc.

She was someone I had had very fruitful business relations with sometime in the past. We however lost contact after I left my former employers. Two years after we lost contact, I chanced on her one day in town. Naturally, I was quite excited to see her, just as she was to see me. The conversation, as expected, went into how her business was. I also wanted to know how her relationship was with the company where we had first met.

The first thing she told me was that she had severed ties with that bank and that she had moved to another bank where she was being treated very well. I was not too happy to hear that she had stopped doing business with that financial institution but I was happy that her business was doing well, all the same. We spoke for some time about business and just as we were about to part ways, she said something that I found interesting.

She started talking about the relationship manager of her account with her new bankers and for a minute, I was "envious" of this gentleman, though I did not know him. This lady was so happy just talking about him. She delivered such a glowing testimonial about her relationship manager that I was moved. But one thing she said that stuck in my mind was this: *"He knows our business so well that we do not take any decision concerning our finances without involving him."* That was it!

I would congratulate this gentleman if I ever get to know and meet him. He had successfully gotten himself so well embedded into the business of his customer that the customer feels a need to get him involved anytime a decision about money is to be taken. That is CUSTOMER INTIMACY!

Gerald A. Abrahams, a renowned speaker on America's public speaking circuit and the head of US-based *Thermo Electron's* Process Instruments Division, provides a good definition of the concept of customer intimacy, albeit a very academic one:

**Customer intimacy** *can be defined as the formal or informal set of relationships established between supplier and customer, with a diverse array of partners, from corporate leadership to functional leadership (engineering, marketing, operations, maintenance, or service) and end-users of products or services.*

There is another definition that some of us prefer because it is simple enough to resonate well at our level of understanding.

**Customer Intimacy** *is the state of knowing your customers REALLY well in ways that can help you serve them better.*

The concept of *Customer Intimacy* has been around for close to two decades. It was first used in an article by Michael Treacy and Fred Wiersema in the Harvard Business Review in January 1993. In the article headlined, *Customer Intimacy and Other Value Disciplines*, the authors wrote about what they referred to as the *three paths to market leadership*. These three paths were namely: *Operational Excellence*, *Product Leadership* and *Customer Intimacy*.

Treacy and Wiersema explained that for an organisation to become a leader in its market it had to deliver superior customer value based on one of those paths. Experts assert that a successful company is one that focuses relentlessly on one of these areas in order to be the best in that area, whilst being, at least, industry average in the other two disciplines.

At the risk of coming across as too academic, I will briefly run through the definitions for each of these areas.

**Operational Excellence:**

*A business strategy in which a company provides products that are neither the best nor the worst on the market, but with the best price and the most convenience for customers.*

Companies that lead in this area concentrate on cost management and optimising their existing operational processes.

**Product Leadership:** This refers to the business strategy in which businesses focus on bringing out newer and more innovative products as a way of staying ahead of the competition. Companies that lead in this area make price and service secondary matters.

This leaves us with the last, but definitely not the least, of the three disciplines identified in the Treacy-Wiersema Value-Discipline model—**Customer Intimacy,** which has already been defined above.

**Why get closer**

I am convinced that of all the three paths, Customer Intimacy is the way to go. It establishes what one writer calls a "virtuous circle." A business gets to REALLY know its customers and this enables it serve the customers better. The customers appreciate the better service and this draws them closer to the business. The closer association results in the business getting to know more about the customers and this enables the business to serve the customers better. This is the cycle that can go on and on. Customer Intimacy makes business sense and should be pursued by all.

As a matter of fact, the times in which we find ourselves calls for a company-wide adoption of the Customer Intimacy Strategy. In these times, when competitors are prepared to go all lengths to "snatch" a customer from the jaws of another, it is more than important that businesses draw closer to their customers.

We are told that it is cheaper to retain existing customers than it is to win new ones. However, customer retention is a function of how well the business gets to know the customer. The success of customer retention is determined by the strength of the relationship between the business and the customer, and this strength is related to how close the customer feels towards the business.

Another reason why Customer Intimacy must become an accepted strategy at the highest level of the organisation is that by getting close to its customers, a business is able to do a better segmentation and targeting of the customers. This will result in better promotional tactics which will in turn result in a reduction in marketing costs wastage.

The more intimate a business is with its customers, the greater the chances of coming out with products and services that will be to the taste of its customers. An early identification of unsatisfied needs has the potential of earning a company a long-term sustainable competitive advantage as the business could come out with a product that will become a leader in its industry. In this instance, one can say that *Customer Intimacy* and *Product Leadership* have been achieved.

Customer Intimacy can also result in increased sales as it allows for easy cross-selling of the company's products and services that the customer might otherwise have gone elsewhere to purchase.

Adopting Customer Intimacy also has benefits for the customer. When a business makes it a policy to get to know its customer well and to do what the customer desires, it results in customer confidence in that business which will ultimately result in greater satisfaction. In short, it makes life easier for the customer.

This was the exact feeling my good friend conveyed to me when we met. The bank had done a great work by becoming "intimate" with her business. She believed that things were now under control. She was in control of the affairs of her business, which, when one thinks of it, is what all business folks are looking for—control over their affairs.

## How to get closer

The key ingredient in getting "intimate" with customers is appropriate INFORMATION. Just as in any relationship, there is a need to obtain information and to communicate that information well. Businesses need to know that creating intimacy with customers must be a conscious effort on the part of the business. It is the job of the business to initiate the closer relationship.

In other words, the dialogue must start with the business. This allows the business to not only give out information, but to also gather information from the customer. The information gathered will reveal otherwise unknown facts about the customer's preferences, needs, wants and behavioural patterns.

## Gather information

Every business has some information about its customers. However, to get closer, there is a need to go beyond just the obvious and dig deeper. The big fishes are found in the deeper waters, so if you need to develop an intimacy that your competitors cannot replicate, you need to do a lot more digging. Every customer interaction is an opportunity to improve customer intimacy and that is why it is important that contact employees are well-taught in the art of asking the right questions.

I have come to realise that many businesses do not even need to do too much digging because they have goldmines of data sitting in their offices begging to be recognised. There are valuable data available on file and we are doing nothing about them. Customer details, payment history, account activity and patterns of activity are a few of the available data sources that businesses can begin digging in.

## Integrate the information

I have found this to be a huge challenge for many businesses. They already possess enough information to develop the level of intimacy with their customers that we have been discussing. However, the problem is that the information is "all over the place." There is no coordination across the organisation from the different sources of data on customers. When systems are put in place that glean information about the customer each and every time the customer interacts with the business, then customer intimacy is just right around the corner.

## Manage the information

Information, like water in a bottle, can get stale over time. That is why it is important that the customer information is kept as fresh as possible. On a regular basis, the business needs to contact the information to ensure that the information is up-to-date. There are firms that possess mountains of data about their clients but the unfortunate issue is that much of that information is of low quality or of no quality at all. It is embarrassing to visit a customer only to be told by neighbours that they have moved from that locality three months prior.

I almost had that unfortunate experience recently. An advertising firm I had some relationship with was planning to move and I had absolutely no idea. Why? I had not contacted them in a while. I was just lucky to have contacted them the previous week for the CEO to inform me of their intended move. You cannot get intimate with someone you do not regularly contact.

**Analyse the information**

Having quality data is not an end in itself; it should be the starting point for building the intimate relationship. Quality information is of no use if it does not lead to customer intimacy. The information must be critically assessed to bring out facts about the customer that can help the business get closer to the customer.

**Use the Information**

For instance, it should not take too much for a bank or any other financial institution to gather so much information about a good customer including the car the customer drives, the year of manufacture, the make and any other details about the auto insurance on the car. If such a customer was to walk in just around the time the insurance on his car was going to expire, the bank could easily cross-sell a *Bancassurance* product to the one.

I could go on and on about the various ways we can make use of the quality information we gather from customers. But I hope I was able to, in the very least, get you thinking about adopting customer intimacy as a strategy for your company, department, unit or desk. As we have seen, customer intimacy can be a very viable option for sustaining one's position in the marketplace and so should not be taken lightly. It pays to be very close to your customers because, just like the tag line for my favourite toothpaste brand goes, THE CLOSER, THE BETTER!

# CHAPTER 10
## *SAYING THE RIGHT THINGS RIGHT*

**Customer Service Implications of Polite Speech**

*"Politeness is the flower of humanity."*

(Joseph Joubert, French philosopher)

Two friends entered a lingerie shop in a popular mall to get some items. According to one of the ladies, she was overweight at the time but as expected, all the items on display were made for ladies of slimmer body shapes. She was so disappointed that she remarked: *"They shouldn't be so discriminatory. They should make this in our size!"* Just as she turned to leave with her friend, the manager of the shop retorted: *"Maybe if you lose some weight, we will have things that will fit you!"*

**"Politeness is the act of choosing among your thoughts."** (Madame de Stael, *Swiss author*)

A visibly-shaken woman walked into a banking hall to lodge a complaint. From her demeanour, it was obvious that she was really worried. She approached the Branch Operations Manager and reported that a withdrawal had been made on her account without her knowledge. She had walked into the bank that morning to withdraw some money but had been informed that she did not have that much in her account. The Operations Manager readily went into the woman's account and reported to her that the withdrawal had been done with an ATM card.

The woman vehemently denied ever using her ATM card on the said day. Initial investigation also revealed that the withdrawal had been in a different branch of the bank. The woman denied ever visiting that town during the period the withdrawal was supposed to have taken place. The manager asked her to put her complaint in writing so that the matter could be investigated thoroughly. She duly obliged and bid the Manager farewell. But just as she walked out, she heard someone pass this comment: *"If you have gone to withdraw your money and have forgotten, don't come and worry us!"*

**"It is wise to apply the oil of refined politeness to the mechanism of friendship."** (*Sidonie-Gabrielle Colette, French novelist and performer*)

An old lady walked into a book shop to get a particular book for one of her grandchildren. She approached the lady at the customer service podium and gave the title of the book to her. The old lady then asked where she could find that particular book. The clerk at the podium waved her arm in the direction of the children's book section and said, *"Over there!"* As the lady walked over to the children's book section, the customer service rep turned to one of her colleagues and said, *"She didn't even try to find it on her own!"*

**"Politeness wins the confidence of princes."** (Chinese Proverb)

A customer sat in front of a customer service rep in a banking hall. He was contending a withdrawal that had been made on his account on a particular day. He claimed that he was not in the country that day so there was no way he could have made that withdrawal. The customer service rep therefore had to take his time to go through the man's account. This process took quite a bit of time which frustrated both customers who were waiting in line and the Branch Operations Manager, whose banking hall was getting choked with angry customers.

After a while, the Branch Operations Manager had had enough. *"What is happening?"* she blurted out to the gentleman manning the front desk. The gentleman excused himself from the customer and went over to explain to the Operations Manager. He came back and still continued his investigations. After about a minute or two, the Branch Operations Manager hollered at the front desk officer, *"But how much is the money that was withdrawn?"* The officer duly responded, *"Madam, please, it was GH 200.00!"* The Manager, in a very sarcastic tone, retorted (in a local language): *"Ah! So it's only GH 200.00 . . . . and we are being bothered like that?!"*

**"Politeness is to human nature what warmth is to wax."** (Arthur Schopenhauer, German philosopher)

An 18-year old had just lost his mother to lung cancer. The deceased had bought some clothes before her demise—clothes that she never wore. In fact, she had not even removed the tags from the clothes. The chap decided to send the clothes back to the store the mother bought them from for a possible refund. When he got there, he approached a cashier who wanted the receipts that were given to the woman. The young man responded that he did not have the receipts to which the cashier rudely responded: *"Why can't you just get the receipt from your mum?"* The bereaved chap told the cashier that his mum was dead.

The cashier gave the guy a stern look and said, "*Well, you do not look too sad about it!*"

**"For me politeness is the sine qua non of civilization."** (Robert A. Heinlein, American science fiction writer)

A consultant had just flown into town and had gotten herself checked into a hotel. The next morning, she called the front desk and asked if the hotel could get her a taxi to an appointment. She was told that the hotel could arrange that. In fact, it was part of the hotel's offers to customers. When the cab arrived, the consultant boarded and gave the driver the address of her destination. However, the driver refused to go until the woman gave him her room number. The consultant was not comfortable giving her room number to a total stranger. The taxi driver claimed that was the norm. He had to charge the fare to the woman's room so that it could be added to her total bill. The woman refused and got out of the cab. She went back to the hotel's reception to lodge a complaint. The taxi driver also followed her into the reception.

After the consultant had narrated her displeasure and discomfort of giving her room number to a complete stranger, the receptionist turned to the taxi driver and without warning said, "*Sir, her room number is 210!*" The consultant was shocked! How could the receptionist do that? She lost her temper and started giving the receptionist a piece of her mind. The receptionist's response was that there was nothing wrong with what she had done. According to her, nothing had ever happened to any customer. She defended the professionalism of the taxi cab drivers that they did business with. The customer would have none of that. But just as she was talking, the receptionist stopped her and rudely asked: "*Are you going to argue with me or are you going to get in the cab?*"

**"If you have no money; be polite." (Danish proverb)**

A guy wanted to give his girlfriend a treat and so he took her out to a very popular restaurant for dinner. According to the fellow, the food at the place was good and indeed they really enjoyed it. After they had eaten, the lady excused herself and went to freshen up inside the ladies. The guy took the opportunity to walk to the counter to pay the bill before the lady returned. When the lady returned, she asked that they spend a few minutes chatting before they left. The place was not full and there were empty tables so the guy obliged and they sat down just to chat.

In less than ten minutes, a waiter approached them and asked if everything was alright. They told him that everything was fine. However, before they could even thank him for asking, the waiter blurted out: *"But sir, if you have finished eating . . . you people must leave. I have to prepare the table for other guests!"*

**"Treat everyone with politeness, even those who are rude to you—not because they are nice, but because you are."** (Author Unknown)

Talking comes naturally to most of us. We just open our mouths and the words begin to come out. Just like with breathing, we do not give too much thought to how we are able to talk. The mechanism of how we are able to produce audible sounds that make sense to the next person is not one that we bother ourselves with.

Many times, though, we are advised to give some thought to the words that come out of our mouths. The tongue can really get us into trouble if we do not tame it. The Good Book warns us against that small muscle in our buccal cavity. American poet and author Anthony Liccione once said, *"A tongue is about the size of a bullet, but much more fierce and powerful."*

The importance of heeding to the advice on thinking about what we want to say before opening our mouths is universal. But we must be extra careful when it comes to dealing with customers. We might get away with making silly and insensitive statements when we are with friends and close acquaintances. However, when we make thoughtless statements in the course of dealing with customers, then we stand a great chance of being in real trouble. Many customer-handling business professionals have lost their jobs just for making those uncaring statements to customers. They allowed their tongues to run faster than their brains, and that is mostly the end result.

We are all well aware of the importance of keeping our customers happy. We know happy customers are repeat buyers and that means more business. It is therefore important that business leaders and supervisors ensure that customer-handling professionals are trained on how to keep their customers happy. One sure way of keeping customers happy is by keeping one's tongue in check.

The 16th century Scottish diplomat, Member of Parliament, poet and philosopher, William Drummond advises: *"Put a bridle on thy tongue; set a guard before thy lips, lest the words of thine own mouth destroy thy peace . . . on much speaking cometh repentance, but in silence is safety."* Those who deal with customers on a regular basis should be circumspect whenever they open their "traps." It is better not to say anything at all than to say, and later, pay!

# CHAPTER 11
## *EXPRESSIONS OF LOVE*

*"I like not only to be loved, but also to be told I am loved."*

George Eliot, English Victorian novelist

### The Little Things Matter

One of the few lessons I learnt from my marriage counsellor, during the preparations for my wedding, was that I was never to forget the little things that really make the big differences in a love affair. For example, the not-too-expensive little gifts, surprise outings, occasional 'I Love You' messages, little pecks here and there, an occasional hug and the likes. According to this counsellor, these little things might be so little to me but very important in the eyes of the lady I was to establish a lifetime partnership with. I must say that sticking to this advice, albeit not always, has helped me a lot in this lifetime journey.

In much the same way, retaining a customer over the course of a lifetime requires that businesses stick to doing the very little things which really matter to their customers. It is these little actions that enhance service magic and sustain customer loyalty. It is good for all businesses to remember that their customers are some other business' prospects.

Customers have plenty of competitors attempting to woo them—some more effectively than others. What differentiates a business is the extent to which it would go to express its love to its customer. What are some of these actions that bring about service excellence which will seem magical in the customer's eyes? What are the little things that companies do that keep the romance going?

### Dedication from the Head

In most of my readings on great companies, one thing I realised that ran through all of their setups is an undying commitment on the part of top management to satisfy the customer. Intense dedication on the part of senior management to be wholly customer-oriented and to lead by example is the key to service excellence. In short, management should exude customer service excellence.

Exceptional service should not only be written out and passed down to staff to run with. Staff must see management "walking the talk." Top management must be seen as treating customers in ways that make them feel truly special. In Disney World, it is reported that once every year top management get to mingle with customers for a whole week. The boss could decide to don a Mickey Mouse costume and sell popcorn and serve out ice creams to visitors, kids and adults alike.

Another example comes to mind concerning a bank that surprised clients when top management "invaded" the banking hall one day to serve customers. I also recall an incident when the Managing Director of a leading furniture retail shop came from his office to take me around his premises even though I was just there to make enquiries. That is what I refer to as walking the talk when it comes to customer service.

For customer romance to blossom in any company, the love affair must be recognised, celebrated and maintained from the top. This customer orientation philosophy will then percolate all the way down to the doorman or sanitation officer. An attitude to serve customers better than all competitors must start from the top.

### Trained to Love

One area where this attitude will be felt is in the area of human capital development. It is no coincidence that smart businesses are known to have stringent training regimes for all staff regardless of their levels or portfolios. How well is management committed to developing the staff to be able to better serve customers? Great and exceptional businesses back their customer orientation philosophy with an intensive training regime.

Once again, IBM stands tall in this light. Peters and Waterman, Jr write that at IBM basic sales training is fifteen months. Of this period 70% is said to be in a branch whilst the rest of the time is spent in university-like settings. It is sad that many companies frown at the idea of spending money to train their staff, especially sales and customer care personnel, on modern ways of relating to customers.

### True Love from Within

Excellent companies know that to achieve excellent external customer service they must necessarily achieve internal customer satisfaction. Such organisations know that customer relations are directly related to employee relations. Great companies have been known all over the world to go to all lengths to ensure that their employees are made to feel right. They know that the first law of customer satisfaction is to treat employees well.

It is a known fact that how a business treats its internal customers is the way those internal customers will treat the external customers. This can be likened to the way your sweetheart will be treated by your family members if you do not respect those same family members. You should not be too shocked if you come to hear that your loved one paid you a visit but was coldly received if you had not conducted yourself well in a lively and pleasant manner at home on the morning of that visit. It is a must that those employees who come into constant contact with customers should be made to feel empowered to serve customers with utmost care and courtesy. This is the one sure way you can expect customer service encounters to be turned into magical moments of romance.

### The Little Fights Spice the Romance

To keep the romance going on in any relationship, it is important that disagreements are sorted out as quickly as possible before situations degenerate into something unbearable.

> **"Customers don't expect you to be perfect. They do expect you to fix things when they go wrong."**
>
> —*Donald Porter V.P., British Airways*

Answering every customer complaint within hours is a time-tested tradition in great companies. IBM is known to answer any customer complaints within twenty-four hours. Ricoh Americas Corporation, makers of Lanier brand of word processing equipment, is reported to deal with any customer issues within four hours. Resolving complaints quickly and courteously has its own benefits such as saving money by eliminating unnecessary additional contacts that escalate costs and also boosting customer confidence. How readily are customer complaints dealt with in your company? Are customers punished for daring to report issues they are not happy with?

**"Customer complaints are the schoolbooks from which we learn."**

*—Unknown*

Romantic companies encourage all staff to collect and report complaints. All complaints are then funnelled into a centralised database. Romantic companies do not consider reception of customer complaints as negative interruptions to doing business. They solicit for complaints because they are aware that expressions of grievances provide opportunities to rectify problems and provide constructive ideas for improving products. When complaints are lodged romantic companies respond to them quickly and by so doing, deepen the romance. It has been found out that customers reward companies that quickly solve problems by remaining loyal to the business.

What if the customer does not complain? Does that mean all is well? According to experts this is not necessarily so. Absence of complaints is not proof of highly satisfied customers. It has been found out that only one out of 25 dissatisfied customers will express dissatisfaction because as a matter of fact most customers don't complain; 50 percent just go away.

Readers will agree with me that in most situations where they have not been too impressed with a product or service, they preferred to walk away without complaining. I always insist that the most dangerous customers are those that do not complain. These dissatisfied customers, it has been found out, will tell 9 to 12 other people how bad the service or product was, whilst satisfied customers will only tell approximately 4 to 5 others of their positive experience.

**Lovers Listen**

**"Spend a lot of time talking to customers face to face. You'd be amazed how many companies don't listen to their customers." Ross Perot**

Romantic companies know how to listen to their customers. These companies know that for a relationship to blossom it is important that the lines of communication are opened at both sides. How many companies do you see in some parts of the world like Africa with toll-free numbers for customers to call in with their ideas or complaints? It is ironic that business leaders will agree that listening is of utmost importance in personal relationships but fail to bring the same sort of reasoning into the business world.

As in every meaningful relationship, the benefits of effectively listening to one's customers are enormous. Studies into the operations of excellent companies reveal that customer complaints and ideas are a vital source of product innovation and improvement ideas. A famous example of product improvement achieved through listening to customers was Levi's steel-riveted jeans. It is reported that Levi obtained the idea from one of its customers, Joseph Youphes from Nevada.

It makes sense to listen to the users of your products for ideas on how to improve those same products. Romantic companies draw their customers closer into the companies. They rely on their customers to provide them with better products and services. These companies know how to listen to customers about their products and proactively seek to redress issues concerning their cherished customers. If you want to know how to please a loved one, listen. By listening, you are able to know what the person wants. Listening is the first step in the all-important process of creating and sustaining empathy. Lack of active, sincere and wholehearted listening is a definite barrier to intimacy between a company and its customers.

> **"To my customer, I may not have the answer, but I'll find it. I may not have the time, but I'll make it."**—*Unknown*

Customer Romance does not just happen; neither is it dependent on just providing product or service for customers, nor is it a puzzling set of practices. Rather, it occurs as a result of a deliberate, thoughtful plan of action. Companies that are known to provide the best customer experiences have philosophies that guide them to take actions their competitors do not even dream of.

One of such mind-sets is this: Excellent companies act as if they are on the verge of losing each and every customer every day. Every business can (and should) woo each customer in a way that makes them want to come back for more. That is the essence of customer romance. Customer loyalty is the single most important key to a company's longevity and ability to provide secure jobs and pay increases. However customer loyalty, like a lover's loyalty, is only a by-product of keeping a good romance going.

# CHAPTER 12
## *A RECIPE FOR SWEET ROMANCE*

*"I'm not an amazing cook. But I can follow a recipe!"*

Rachel McAdams, *Canadian actress*

Ken stood in the kitchen for what seemed like an eternity. He really wanted to impress Gifty, his new found love, with her favourite meal. She had promised him that she was coming back that afternoon and so Ken wanted to surprise her. The first thing he had done that morning was to place a call to the one person he knew was an expert in preparing that meal—his sister. She gave him a list of ingredients he needed but not before asking why her brother wanted the list. Ken had brushed aside the second question with an excuse. Fortunately for him, he already had every single item on the list. He had even taken each item out and arranged them on the shelf. All that was left was for him to begin the actual cooking.

But contrary to his expectations things were not going too well. He had everything he needed to prepare the meal with the exception of one very important ingredient—the knowhow! Ken had forgotten to ask his sister for the specific details of how to prepare the meal. He was stuck and he needed to act fast. Time was not on his side.

He weighed his options. He could either rush out to get the meal from a restaurant in town or he could go ahead and prepare it using his own "wisdom." He instantly decided against the latter. That could result in a culinary catastrophe. He could end up feeding her something not meant to be consumed by humans. There was a third option, though. He could call the sister and confess that he was attempting to cook for Gifty and was struggling. But that would be the last thing he would do. The teasing that would accompany that option was something Ken was not ready to endure. It seemed the first option was the best.

Rushing into his room, he grabbed his car keys and made a beeline for the garage. Just as he was about to drive out, the bell rang. His heart missed a beat. "This shouldn't be her," he prayed. He stealthily walked to the main gate and peeked through the peephole. His jaw dropped. Luckily, it was not Gifty. It was his sister. What was she doing there at that time? She never mentioned that she was passing by. The questions raced through Ken's mind as he opened the gates for her. As she walked in, she smiled and, in her teasing voice, said, "You are attempting to cook for Gifty. Are you not?"

While many businesses desire to just acquire good customers, smart businesses seek to create strong customer romance. They know it is all about reaching the hearts of customers so they are ready to cook up the best of experiences for their customers. Average companies treat customers as statistics but excellent companies treat customers as lives. Smart businesses strive to always stay on the minds of their customers. They know that to be close to a customer, they must sometimes get out of their comfort zones and do things that will surprise their customers.

Like Ken, you could have the right idea as to what to do to please the special someone. You might be lucky enough to have all the right ingredients. The challenge then becomes how one can combine all the right ingredients in the right mixture to create that right experience. Without a recipe book, the inexperienced cook like Ken might struggle. Master Chefs do not need to refer to any cook book. It is all in their heads. Experience has taught them what quantities to put in at what time. But for beginners it is important to resort to a guide.

What then is that guide, that recipe for making a customer fall in love with your offering? Can the seemingly complicated process of romance be reduced to a simple equation? Experts in the psychology of love believe this can be done. They are of the opinion that anyone can be made to fall in love with another person if the right steps are followed. They, however, acknowledge that the process can still be quite complicated and should be taken seriously if the best results are to be obtained.

## All relevant information

The first step in developing good customer romance is obtaining vital information about prospective buyers/dealers prior to initiating the move. Information gathering is an important part of the process of developing intimate relationships with customers. A failure to look below the surface is the root cause of much of the frustration that customers go through in their dealings with businesses. Not gathering enough information about one's customers can lead to discriminatory or prejudicial attitudes and overly trivial evaluations that wreak havoc on the romance.

I am sure many readers will remember a time when they had to do such a thorough investigation on someone they had become besotted. I believe your investigative skills would make even Sherlock

Holmes green with envy. I know of lovesick guys who would even pay money for information on ladies from their friends, just to know what to say when they got the chance to speak to the person. Such vital pieces of information would prevent a Romeo from buying a red dress for a Juliet whose favourite colour is pink. How would you know her date of birth if you do not undertake a thorough background check?

Gathering in-depth information about customers reveals critical individual differences, which can serve as basis for deepening relationships. Like all humans, customers love to be treated and appreciated as unique individuals and not as statistics. No one wants to be known as Account Number 0987654321 or Project # XC765. If you call your loved ones by their own special names, why would you want to make the one who puts money in your pocket a mere statistical consideration? After gathering all the information you can about the prospect or the customer, it is then time to take the process to the opening stage: creating a good first impression.

**At first sight**

The debate is still on. Does love at first sight really exist? I would not want to wade into that battle, at least not now. It would not serve my purpose. No matter what side of the debate you are on, there is no doubt that when it comes to wooing customers, love seeds are often sown during the first few minutes of the relationship. Customers do not take forever to make up their minds about whether to do business with you or not.

Customers will occasionally try a product many times before they make up their minds on whether to establish a lifetime relationship with that product or not. However, on many occasions the mind of the customer would have been made up within the first few minutes. Just as any two people entering a relationship begin, and continue, to make rapid decisions about their intentions during their first meeting or conversation, so do customers. The first date is always very important to establish a long term relationship.

In much the same way, the kind of first impression customers have about your business is critical for the long-term sustainability of the romance. According to two independent pieces of research, nearly 90% of customers form an impression about how competent and reputable a company is based on what they see when they walk through its doors. For some customers, the first thing they see is the façade of the business, even before they walk through the doors. A way of adding value to a client's experience is by making the facility pleasing and comfortable.

**"Washrooms will always tell if your company cares about its customers."**—*Unknown*

What image does the frontage and surroundings of your business bring to mind? MacDonald's, the international fast food giant, is legendary for the cleanliness of all its eateries around the world. I find some of the buildings appearing on the skyline of some national capitals of African countries very interesting. These buildings, I believe, are sending out a positive message to all their customers, that they are serious players on the international business stage. However, images must be appropriate especially in the market where the company operates. Appropriateness is important. I was telling a former colleague that the reason why his bank's branch was not mobilising enough deposits, was that their building was too imposing for the area it was operating in.

An organisation's image is also carried about as the image of its sales and customer care personnel. If the customer does not come into direct contact with the company, then to the customer the company is the sales professional. Are the appearances of the sales executives of your firm in line with the image the firm wants to project in the market? Employees, especially those that come into regular contact with a firm's customers, are *"walking and talking billboards"* of that firm. In short, appearances matter.

Customers form an impression of a business, based on how the place looks, smells or feels before they even decide to make any business commitment. Any company therefore that is bent on "romancing" its customers should design its premises and dress its sales and customer care personnel to appear confident and competent. Here also, suitability is important. It would be quite an unusual sight to see firewood being sold in glass cages in a shopping mall. I hope you get my meaning.

The attire of the sales professional should help connect with the customer—not separate you from the customer. For example, if a sales executive is calling on factory workers, he or she does not necessarily have to do so in a suit and tie, as that would separate him or her from the workers, and generate a bit of discomfort among those in the "dirty" overalls. Such a sales person would not be dressed appropriately in a way that would relate to the prospects.

**How Nice To See You**

It is not enough to just look good, you must act "good" if you intend to keep the romance going. Any contact with a customer provides fertile ground for giving great customer service. Businesses should teach their frontline staff to treat customers like the special people they are. It is a must that all frontline employees learn to give every service with a smile. Service should always be accompanied with a smile. A smile tells customers that you are always happy to meet them.

It is important to smile while talking to a customer over the phone. A smile can be heard on the other end of the line. It makes you sound friendly and so less threatening. The human voice is a great tool that when used appropriately can help woo a customer for life. Frontline staff should be trained on how to use their voices in a light and friendly manner. This will open the door to the customer's heart. When a customer walks through the door of your business or if you are allowed into the presence of a customer, your main aim should be to make the encounter pleasurable for the customer. Let the person enjoy being in your company.

**Delicate First Love**

**"Early love is a delicate little flower."**

(Leil Lowndes)

As with all things that have to grow, the initial stages of a romantic relationship have to be handled cautiously. Certain behaviour or attitudes that will go undetected or casually tossed aside later in the relationship can eat away at early love. Often, these love poisons could kill the love at once whilst under other conditions they would begin to strangle the life out of the love slowly. Extreme caution should be the watchword at the start of early relationships.

Romantic companies go all lengths to ensure that new customers are treated very well. Average companies go to all lengths to win new customers, and then leave them hanging immediately after the first deal.

Average eateries and restaurants treat their customers as if they would not want them to come back whilst romantic restaurants treat first-time patrons in such a way that they would want to come back for more. Average banks believe customer care ends immediately after the customer opens an account and deposits an amount. Average insurance companies believe after the policy is written their job is done. They then sit back and just wait for the regular payments to come in.

In these competitive times, being average would eventually take you below average. You should not aim for average, you should go for excellent. Being average just gets you by. What you want to do is to be excellent. That is what "romantic" companies do.

**What do I get in return?**

Relationship experts insist that a prerequisite for establishing a long-lasting romantic relationship is to initially convince the other partner that there is a reward for getting into the relationship. Though mostly at an unconscious level, we all enter relationships for what we believe we will get from it. According to Leil Lowndes in her aptly-titled book, *How to Make Anyone Fall in Love with You*, "*lovers unconsciously calculate the other person's comparable worth, the cost-benefit ratio of the relationship, the hidden costs, the maintenance fee, and the assumed depreciation. Then they ask themselves, 'Is this the best offer I can get?'*"

I believe some readers will argue that love is selfless and would give examples of couples who are completely altruistic and are ready to sacrifice for each other. I would not doubt that assertion. However, that kind of love comes in only after the other fellow has fallen in love. From the very beginning it is essential that you communicate to the one that he or she will benefit from the relationship. As Lowndes puts it, "everyone has a market value." The secret therefore is to find what the person would love to receive from the relationship and then go about providing that very thing.

In much the same way, romancing your customer requires that you find out what the customer would love from the relationship and as much as possible provide that. Every customer wants the best possible out of every deal. In this sense, smart businesses know that all customers differ according to their needs and wants. They do not provide blanket "one-size-fits-all" services to all customers. Different sales, marketing or promotional programmes are designed for different segments of the market.

I have found out that every customer has a different request at any point in time. During my days in banking operations, I had customers who preferred to have their statements delivered on a weekly basis, others on a monthly basis and others daily. I remember a time when we decided to give all our large customers weekly statements. One particular customer however rejected the weekly bank statements because he did not like having to deal with so many papers. It confused him during his monthly accounts reconciliation. I then realised that not all customers desire the same things in a business relationship. What fascinates one customer will not move another. What is exceptional customer service in the eyes of one customer is an expected service in the eyes of another.

Relationships thrive on giving, so businesses should know what will interest their customers and then endeavour to give out those things. In the area of giving, however, romantic companies should know where to draw the line. When it is not possible to give customers what they ask for, they should not be made to feel bad. Customers must know that they have been heard. They must feel that they have been treated fairly. Being romantic does not mean you do things to your own detriment. Committed customers can be very empathetic if issues are explained to them well.

## Massaging the Ego

Every person feels special in this life and the key to getting into their world is to celebrate that uniqueness. Experts advise that to win someone's love there is a need for thorough understanding of the person's self-image and then move ahead to foster it. Self-images are distinct characteristics that have to be supported. Feeding your partner's ideal self-image is critical for the creation and sustenance of a long-lasting relationship. If you can make your partner feel that you are the kind of person who will love them for who they are, and not for what they possess, chances are you have found a love for life.

I have come to realise that customers love companies that make them feel good about themselves—companies that reflect what they, the customers, believe about themselves. Customers fall in love with the company that says to them, "*You are unique. You are great. We are the only ones who can make you feel that way. Fall in love with us and we will continue to make you feel great.*"

Every one we meet in this life desires recognition, among other wants, and our ability to present ourselves as sole providers of their desires greatly enhances our chances of winning their hearts. Romantic companies tend to meet the emotional desires of their clients. Customers, like spouses, can be at your beck and call if you give them what they need, when they need it and how they need it. Massage their ego and you have them by the heart.

## Turn on the Razzle-Dazzle

Relationship experts advise that to maintain a romantic relationship there is a need for an occasional surprise gift from loved ones. However, to keep the love froth steaming, one must do more. To keep your loved one almost always in the mood for the love, it is important to take the magic some levels higher. This is what I refer to as turning on the "razzle-dazzle."

If you were to ask me what specific things one needs to do to turn on the magic in a relationship, I would not be able to offer you a satisfactory answer. I am not a relationship expert; I am into customer care. What I will tell you is to use your imagination.

One way I subscribe to when it comes to dazzling your precious one is to put yourself in the person's shoes. What wonderful thing would you not expect to be done for you? Then do that. What is it that your loved one would not expect you to do? What can you do that will send your dear love into fits of ecstasy?

Any business that really wants to woo its customers and maintain them for a lifetime must know how to thrill them. Smart businesses know how to turn the romance on at the right time for their customers. This results in the business snatching a larger market share from their competitors. Romantic companies know how to offer magical customer care.

Magical customer service occurs when customers perceive they are receiving service that is above and beyond what they were expecting. The customers receive acts of spontaneous service that delight them. As a result, they become advocates for your business, promoting the business by telling others about their magical experience. This is where the importance of the information gathered at the first stage of the affair becomes useful.

What prevents a firm I deal with from sending me a surprise birthday gift or message? What is the use of all the personal details they collected from me? The forms and documents that clients fill out when entering a business deal are a mine of useful information but it would take a romantic company to dig deep and to put that information to good use.

I recently got a text message from an insurance company I had stopped doing business with because of the unprofessional nature of the salesman who sold me the policy. Although as far as I was concerned our relationship was over, it still intrigued me that they were able to contact me via SMS. I believe if they had been sending me these messages whilst I was still actively doing business with them, I might have ignored their poor salesman and stayed with them.

A simple thank you note does not cost a lot but does wonders to the mindset customers have about their companies.

> *"There is no honest woman with an uncorrupted heart whom a man is not sure of conquering by dint of gratitude."* Giacoma Casanova.

Companies have been known to send clippings of newspaper and magazine articles they believe would be of interest to their clients as gifts. This has been known to mesmerise clients and kept them glued to those caring companies.

# CHAPTER 13
## *A LABOUR OF LOVE*

**Customer Service and the Emotional Labour Theory**

*"Nothing is born into this world without labor."*

Rob Liano, *Author and Life Coach*

Amina has a smile that will melt your heart. Standing at 1.4 metres, she radiates a beauty that transcends her looks. Her bubbly character is accentuated by her infectious laughter. Seeing her playing under the large neem trees that flank the road to the city centre, she comes across as the average teenager—excitable, carefree and full of life. But Amina is not. Amina is referred to in the West African country of Ghana as a *"kaya yoo"*, that is a female porter. Her job is to carry heavy loads on her head for a paltry fee. Most days, Amina gets to the little shack she shares with three of her friends all weak and worn out.

Amina has a difficult life. Her job exacts so much physical strength from her young body. But she must work if she is to survive on the unforgiving streets of Accra. One might not dare to compare what frontline employees do on a daily basis, i.e. handling customers, with what Amina does in terms of labour intensity. But some experts would disagree with that.

As a matter of fact, customer service is recognised as one of the jobs that demands lots of labour. Now, you may be wondering—where is the labour in just sitting and smiling to customers? How laborious is it to be nice to people? Customer service executives do not tote heavy loads under the scorching sun. How can they be involved in a laborious work? Interestingly, researchers believe that jobs that involve dealing with people require a lot of effort or labour. They refer to that emotional effort exerted in serving customers as EMOTIONAL LABOUR.

The term was made popular after the 1979 publication of a piece in the *American Journal of Sociology* by Arlie Russel Hochschild, Sociology professor at University of California, Berkeley in the USA. Many other studies have been undertaken on the subject since then. A 1994 study I came across goes further to list various characterisations of Emotional Labour.

In one instance, emotions are seen as products to be sold. This is the case in the activities performed by waiters, stewardesses, and many such jobs. Some have argued that individuals involved in jobs that involve waiting on customers are paid to "sell their emotions." In other words, what the lady at the restaurant is selling to you is a combination of good salad, fruit juice and a great smile. What the flight attendant is selling is a smooth journey to your destination plus a warm feeling.

Diane M. Monaghan defined Emotional Labour in a 2006 dissertation as such:

*"the effort involved in performing emotional regulation for the purpose of complying with the interpersonal demands required*

*in order to perform a job in an organization and in order to produce an organizationally sanctioned emotional response."*

Admittedly, that definition is a bit convoluted but it makes perfect sense when you think of it. Emotional Labour is simply the addition of our emotions or feelings to the work we do as customer service professionals. When you encounter a customer and you have to alter your emotions to enable you offer the best of service, you are providing emotional labour. When an angry customer is giving you a piece of his or her mind and you just manage to control yourself without also resorting to invectives, you are providing emotional labour.

As a matter of fact, you might not be toting a pan of concrete on your head, but you are still providing labour. Granted, physical labour is not for the faint-hearted but neither is emotional labour. At any point in an interaction with a customer, chances are that you are in labour because you are actually "forcing" yourself to do something that is not congruent with what you would have normally done. If you have had any experience at the frontline, you will definitely understand what I am talking about. You are forced by the conditions you find yourself in to act in a way that you would normally not have acted. The force you have applied to stay calm is Emotional Labour.

Being nice for a few minutes might be taken for granted but to stay sweet and nice for a whole day is tough. Now consider the fact that you are expected to stay nice not for just a day, or a week or a month or even a year, but for years. This is a real cracker.

## Kinds of Emotional Labour

There are two recognised forms of Emotional Labour, i.e. *surface acting* and *deep acting*. In a piece published in a 2003 edition of the Academy of Management Journal, Alicia Grandey of Penn State University defined Surface Acting as simply modifying one's facial expression and Deep Acting as actually modifying inner feelings.

Diane M. Monaghan, however, goes a bit deeper. She defines Surface Acting as a concentration "on the external display of emotion." Faking a smile when you are having a bad headache on a Friday afternoon when you are hungry and there is an angry customer in front of you will definitely qualify as Surface Acting. That display is only superficial and will therefore count as Surface Acting.

Deep Acting, on the other hand, involves a deliberate attempt to change any emotions you might be feeling. It is one thing to fake a smile even when you are really ticked off and it is another thing to make every conscious effort to change the way you actually feel. The example Monaghan gives for Deep Acting is focusing one's mind on a positive past experience in the middle of a potentially negative encounter with a customer just to ensure that you do not lose control of your emotions.

The two kinds of emotional labour must however be seen in the light of what Grandey refers to as *genuine expression of emotion*. This happens when an employee's emotions are exactly what are required of the person to perform whatever work is expected of the one. For instance, you expect a teller to be cheerful and welcoming to customers. If a teller leaves her house and comes to work already feeling great and happy, her genuine emotions are just what her job requires. In this instance, such a teller is not experiencing any labour, according to Grandey. The emotions she is experiencing come to her without any effort and so there is actually no labour. At any one time, a customer service professional might be engaging in Surface Acting, Deep Acting, or be expressing genuine emotions or a combination of all three.

Of all the reading I have done on this subject, one aspect that piques my interest is the different levels of labour that various individuals might exert doing the same job. For instance, in a typical bank you will come across more than one teller. In most cases, there will be between three and five. Each and every one of these tellers is unique in his or her own emotional make-up. There are some that have naturally sunny dispositions while for others, it might take some effort to get them to smile.

It would be easier to measure the amount of emotional labour each teller exerts in an average day and compare all of their efforts if they deal with customers with similar emotional composition. However, you and I know that this is not the case. Different tellers will face different customers with different emotional make-ups. What this means is that on an average day, some tellers will be called on to exert more emotional labour than others. Therefore at the end of the day, some will be more drained than others. This brings me to my next point . . .

**Emotional Exhaustion**

As the labourer on the farm or at the construction site becomes tired at the end of the day, so does the customer service executive; thus, the term, *Emotional Exhaustion*. It is in this state that individuals are most at risk of losing their cool. Supervisors and managers must be able to detect when their staff, especially those on the frontline are emotionally drained. Experts tell us that when we see signs of anxiety, nervousness, frustration and easy irritability, then we might be seeing an individual whose emotional strength is almost drained out. Emotional exhaustion also has some physical effects that one can detect such as fatigue, headaches, spinal pains and so on.

If we begin to view emotions as products, then we will make every effort to keep our emotions fresh regularly, just as we would a product. Stress management techniques are therefore very important for frontline employees. They need these techniques if their emotions are to stay fresh.

I believe this Emotional Labour idea is something that managers and supervisors must take very seriously. Chances are we might not be fielding our very best staff at the frontline. We might be placing individuals at the frontline whose emotions are so far off from what are needed to give our customers the great service that they need.

For those of us in the line of fire, we are being asked to express genuine emotions that are in line with what the job expects of us. If for some reason we cannot be genuine, we are allowed to fake it as in *Surface Acting* or better still go deep down to change our emotions positively as in *Deep Acting*. So if today, you encounter a customer who is really pushing you to the wall and you are doing all that you can to stay calm, never forget that you are in labour. Hang in there.

# CHAPTER 14
## *THE ODOUR OF CANDOUR*

**The Consequences of Deception**

*"You can't leave a footprint that lasts if you're always walking on tiptoe."*

*Marion Blakey, American Adminsitrator*

In the year 2009, a popular Israeli clothing store *Castro and Fox*, together with other companies, was hit with a heavy fine by Israel's Ministry of Industry, Trade and Labour for deceiving customers through deceptive advertising. An in-depth analysis of the case makes for very interesting reading.

Among other things, *Castro and Fox* was faulted for claiming that they were having a 50-per cent-off shoe sale, but refused to disclose what specific prices were being cut in half. Interestingly, the prices the store was referring to were old prices from way before the time of the promotion. While customers taught the half-price applied to the most current prices, the store was referring to some other higher prices. This was regarded as deceptive and against Israeli Consumer Laws.

In other circumstances, labelling items as "HOT SALE" was deemed deceptive by authorities who found out that those items had no previous price and that the "HOT" prices were actually the original prices of the products. Therefore, labelling them as "HOT" gave the false impression that prices were being slashed down, which was actually not the case.

Another firm, *Home Center,* was fined because they were asking customers to pay additional shipping fees when ordered items arrived at customers' homes. The law is that the firm should have been forthright with the total cost of the product and not "catch" customers unawares with additional costs.

As I read through the case, I found it interesting that there were some countries whose consumer protection laws were so stringently adhered to—to the extent that companies could not get away with any deceptive practices towards their customers.

I have been thinking. Does not the absence of good Consumer Protection Laws in some countries facilitate the engagement of businesses in the same deceptive practices engaged in by *Castro and Fox*? I very much think so. But will the enactment of a consumer protection law prevent the deception of customers by businesses? I am not sure. In the very least, it will give consumers something to stand on, a legal backing to fall on, when things do not go too well.

Deception of customers will be around for as long as some businesses would want to make a quick windfall. Businesses that do not understand the concept of customer romance will continue to provide misleading information to customers. *Un-romantic* companies are those that try to scam customers out of their hard-earned money. Some will succeed; others will be found out. Things like that will continue with or without a law to protect consumers. But with the eventual passing of these laws, we might be able to punish some of those businesses that have no scruples about such acts.

Some businesses will also get away with their dishonest deeds. How? We, the consumers, will allow them to. We will continue to patronise their goods and services, and by so doing, give them the impression that we do not care if they cheat us or not.

Majority of these businesses that engage in deceptive practices, however, will not get away with their deeds. Consumer power will carry the day. Even if the executives of such businesses are not hauled before the courts, consumers will punish them by not only staying away but also encouraging other consumers to do likewise. That will be the real punishment—not the meagre fines imposed by the courts that will not do much to the bottom-line of those businesses.

When businesses throw away the trust customers have for them, what they also throw away is the possibility of a repeat business. If you know anything about customer lifetime value, you will know that the value a customer brings to a business is not the cost of a one-time purchase. The real value is in the cumulative values of the different transactions over a lifetime of the business relationship. That is where the profit for the business is. So taking advantage of a customer in a single transaction is not only unethical but it does not also make business sense. Truth and honesty are the founding pillars for every serious relationship.

I wish the guy at the car wash I frequently visit was educated enough to have known this. Obviously, his superiors had not taught him that business candour pays more than customer deception. He had not heard Thomas Jefferson, the third US President, say that *"Honesty is the first chapter in the book of wisdom."*

I once paid a visit to the car wash to have my car thoroughly cleaned up because it was in quite a mess—the kind of mess that turns heads on a Monday morning. I did not want colleagues asking me if I had been on a safari during the weekend. Of particular interest to me was the boot of the car (trunk, for my American friends). I needed it really cleaned because I had carried some stuff in the boot that had left bits of paper and dirt in there.

I got to the place around 4 p.m. As expected, the place was packed with other vehicles and so I had to patiently wait for a while. Eventually, a guy approached me. He offered to work on my car after he was done with a Mitsubishi *Pajero* he was working on. After about fifteen minutes, he came over and started working on my vehicle. I sat there and observed as he took out a vacuum cleaner, got inside the car and started working. After a while I saw him get inside the boot and continued what seemed like a good clean up.

After about ten minutes, he beckoned to me to move the vehicle over to the ramp for him to do the external washing. I gladly did that and within thirty minutes, I was out of the place and back home. As far as I knew, everything was fine. I had even given the fellow a big tip for his efforts. Apparently, all was not as fine as I thought.

On Monday morning, I got all dressed up, ready to go to work. I opened the boot of the car and I was shocked to the bone—the boot was as dirty as it was before I sent the car to the wash. I could not believe my eyes. The cleaner had simply hoodwinked me and I had fallen flat for his gimmicks. As I drove to work that morning, I replayed the entire incident in my mind. I had to give it to the guy. He was smart. From the way he faked the whole vacuum cleaning process I was sure that was not the first time he was playing that trick on a customer.

I should have driven by the place that Monday morning to lodge a complaint with his boss, but I decided against that. I was not prepared to go through the hassle. What if I got there and he denied it? Anyway, I decided to take the option many customers would take. I have decided to stop using their services.

It seems every industry has its own unique ways of duping customers. *Castro and Fox* might have been punished for hidden cost but there are other deceptive ways of dealing with customers. We have all heard stories of fuel station attendants filling "air" into fuel tanks in such a way that vehicle fuel gauges did not detect the fraudulent acts until the car had been driven some distance away. We know of conmen wrapping up stones and bars of soap as mobile phones for unsuspecting customers on the streets of some African countries.

We have heard of cases of clauses being hidden within the fine print of contracts that customers will normally not take time to read. When the time comes for customers to get what they believe they are entitled to, they are shown the little prohibitive clause embedded somewhere within the fine print.

Then there are the medicinal products and foods that are given false labels just to entice customers to buy them. There have also been reports from some African countries about market women retailing flour, sugar, maize or rice who will place some material at the bottom of the traditional measuring tin to reduce the quantity of grain customers are entitled to.

There are many other instances where a business has tried to pull a fast one on its customers and had been found out. It beats my mind why businesses do not just act in all honesty towards their customers. After all, there are many benefits that accrue from being honest in business dealings. *All faults may be forgiven of him who has perfect candour,* so says Walt Whitman, American poet and journalist. He was right. When a business remains truthful with its customers, there is always the tendency for its customers to be more forgiving when things do not go too well. For instance, if that bloke at the car wash had told me that he would not have had time to do a good job, I would have understood. Instead, he decided to pull a fast one on me.

What is love without trust? What is Customer Romance without honesty? Many relationships have broken up because someone lied and got caught. Many divorces can be traced to a simple lie. Honesty inspires trust and trust holds relationships together. The concept of Customer Relationship requires businesses to be as open as possible with their customers. It is by so doing that you can win the genuine love of the customer. Lies and deception are eventually found out.

If you are in business and at this moment an opportunity is presenting itself for you to deceive your customers, please think twice before you are tempted to do. You might make money through deceptive practices and you might go scot-free. You might also decide to go with honesty and lose some money. But never forget—the scent of romance is actually the odour of candour and it lingers on and on and on!

# CHAPTER 15
## *WHEN THE ROMANCE TURNS SOUR*

*"To fall in love is awfully simple; to fall out of love is simply awful."*

*Anonymous*

Dan, a business man, came into my office to make some enquiries. During the discussions, he told me a story that really made me appreciate what itinerant business people go through when they travel out of this country to do business. He said that he had to do some business in South Africa and was thinking about how to have all his money in his pocket when he got there. He went to his bankers for some Travellers' Cheques but his bankers thought the better option was to give him an electronic card which had all his money on it. He was assured that when he got to South Africa, all he needed to do was go to any bank with an ATM that could take his card.

The gentleman said he wanted to be sure that what he was being told was true, so he tried the card with another bank in Ghana before he flew out. The card worked well. He got to South Africa and went about his business. He began ordering his goods and enjoying his stay in that wonderful country. It was when it came to the initial payment for his goods that his problems began.

Dan went to a nearby bank that had an ATM that was supposedly compliant with his card. He was in for a shock. The card did not work. He tried everything he could but the ATM did not spew out any cash for the poor man. He said he stood in the cold Johannesburg night and felt like shedding tears.

The next day, Dan called his bankers in Ghana and reported the incident. He was told the only option was for some money to be sent to him via the SWIFT transfer system. He told me that he lodged the complaint on a Friday and so he was sure that, at most, by the next Tuesday he would have received his money for him to go continue his business and come back home to Ghana. Much to his surprise, he stayed in South Africa for more than a week before the money came. By the time the money got to him, he had literally started begging for food from Good Samaritans. To cut a long story short, he had to leave his goods in South Africa and fly back to Ghana.

The anger in his face as he narrated his ordeal was palpable. He told me he had already contacted his lawyers who were planning to take legal action against the bank in question. I advised him against that though, because I had some good friends in that bank. In fact, I had to set up an appointment between this aggrieved customer and the Head of Customer Service of that bank.

After the gentleman left, I sat back and wondered what that bank could do to make this customer happy again. I did not want to be in the shoes of my counterpart in that bank. How was his bank going to recover from this incident? It occurred to me at that moment though that if the service recovery paradox really holds true then there was still hope for that bank in the eyes of this customer.

If you are wondering what this whole service recovery paradox is about, let me attempt to explain. The service recovery paradox postulates that the overall satisfaction levels of recovered customers exceed those of customers who did not encounter any problems with the initial service. Wikipedia explains it as such: *The service recovery paradox states that with a highly effective service recovery, a service or product failure offers a chance to achieve higher satisfaction ratings from customers than if the failure had never happened.*

There is one interesting finding about this Paradox but I will deal with that at the tail end of this chapter. I would first like to take readers through some steps that my colleague at that bank can take to, in the very least, ensure that this customer does not take this matter to unpalatable levels.

## STEP ONE: Accept

Service recovery is effective if it starts with the first person the customer talks to about the problem. Anytime a customer brings an issue before any staff member, regardless of the person's position, department or even job schedule, the onus falls on that particular individual to "own" the issue. Owning the issue does not necessarily mean finding the solution to the problem. Chances are that individual might not have what it takes to get the customer satisfied.

"Owning" the issue is assuring the customer of all your efforts in finding a solution to the problem. I submit that anyone who receives a customer on behalf of a company or picks up the phone on behalf of the company must be seen by the customer as putting in enough effort to find solutions to the problem. It is a crime against customer service and against any company for any member of staff to adopt the "it's not my fault" stance.

## STEP TWO: Apologise

I have come to realize that it is very difficult for many of us to say "sorry" especially when we feel we are not at fault. What we must appreciate, when it comes to service recovery, is that a sincere apology actually works. I have heard some individuals say that they do not see the point in saying "sorry" because an apology does not actually solve the problem. Granted, but you will admit that a sincere heartfelt apology can help defuse a potentially volatile situation.

Apologies are also only effective when they are made sincerely and without any "additions." Many people take business issues too much to heart. When customers approach them with problems, these professionals begin to lie and make excuses. This attitude further muddies the waters. We need to understand that we are standing in for the company and so the company's image must be paramount.

In addition to a sincere apology, staff must learn to be empathetic when customers are frustrated. An apology and empathy combined well make the customer feel understood. When dealing with customers like our friend who got stranded in South Africa, one must use statements and phrases that make customers feel that their issues are being heard.

## STEP THREE: Action

This is a crucial step in the service recovery process. This is where the rubber meets the road. No amount of apology and empathy will suffice if you do not remedy the situation. However, action must be IMMEDIATE if it is to be felt. The last thing you want a dissatisfied customer to do is to wait unnecessarily. Any delay will aggravate the situation. I assert that even when you are on your way to win a new customer and an existing customer calls you with a problem, you must call the new one, apologise and move on to solve the existing customer's problem.

There is that wonderful story of the FEDEX delivery man who trekked through acres of snow just to deliver a package for a customer whose parcel had been delayed. That is what I am talking about. Action must be immediate and must be done at all reasonable cost. Sometimes it even helps to compensate customers when things have not gone too well. It must however be stated that immediate action only works when staff are empowered enough to perform. If frontline employees do not have some measure of authority to satisfy customers, then the business' service recovery might not be up to scratch.

I am sure when businesses take these three simple steps, they will be able to recover from a bad service experience. Their customers will be so happy that the effects of the service recovery paradox will become apparent. I must add however that the service recovery paradox has the potential of making service people slack concerning the delivery of quality. I think it would be unfortunate for business people not to take providing quality service first time seriously.

My "fears" were confirmed when I came across an empirical research paper by two professors Stefan Michel and Matthew L. Meuter. In a paper titled *The Service Recovery Paradox: True but overrated?*, the researchers claimed that they had found evidence that the service recovery paradox exists only under very special conditions. According to the findings of this study, the paradox appears when customers compare a recovery that is *"much better than expected"* with an error-free initial service that is just *"satisfying."*

What this means is that if what the customer experiences on a regular basis is just *satisfying,* then that customer will be totally impressed if a problem arises and in solving the problem he is given *exceptional service.* The study made use of a survey of more than 11,000 customers of a retail bank. What they found rather was that what was most preferred by customers is a very satisfying initial service. Customers want service providers to get it right the first time. Customers are not too keen on you making them angry and then coming back to sort things out exceptionally.

I wonder what the businessman, who suffered such embarrassment in South Africa, would say about the service recovery paradox. I am sure he will readily agree with Michel and Meuter that a great initial service is far better than bad service recovered well. One thing we must never lose sight of is the fact that service recovery should result in systems that will ensure that the same mistakes are not repeated. It is when this is done that we can say that sometimes out of the ashes of bad experiences, some good can arise.

# CHAPTER 16
## *REWARDS OF THE ROMANCE*

*"Love is the master key that opens the gates of happiness."*

Oliver Wendell Holmes, Sr.,
*American physician and poet*

Just as love rewards, so customer romance pays. For years, businesses that have been engaged in customer romance have been reaping the many benefits of this stance while their counterparts and competitors struggle to survive in the market. I have decided to entice you with a few of the beneficial behaviours exhibited by customers that are in love.

**Just to be close to you**

Committed customers are sure to stay close to you. These customers will even ignore certain things the business does which they would not tolerate elsewhere. Even if the business goofs in its offering, committed customers will explain it away as "just one of those days." When the customer feels that they are number one on your list, they will not go to experiment elsewhere; they will stick with what they have and what they enjoy!

I recall days when, as a relationship officer of a bank, I had made some mistakes of omissions which I felt were quite grievous but my committed customers always understood. These customers stuck with me because they remembered times in the past when I had shown so much "love" to them. Smart businesses should go out of their way to initiate a romantic affair with their cherished customers and they should do anything just to be close.

**Don't bother, I will come**

When I began courting the lady who was later to become Mrs J. N. Halm, I would regularly travel from one end of town to get to her house at the other end of town. This went on for months until she finally gave in to my proposal. From then onwards, I had the liberty and luxury of minimising my traverses to her place as she took over and started coming over to my place. I believe many readers will identify with that experience.

One of the key benefits of establishing a good level of customer romance is that you do not have to go over to sell to them; they will come to you when they need a product or service. The cost of maintaining the relationship will be greatly minimised. I recall some journeys we had to make outside town to visit new customers we were trying to woo. However, after the romance began, the customers felt they were bothering us by asking us to travel all the way to their offices. Whenever I contacted them to plan a visit, they would say, "Don't bother, I will rather come." That is a customer in love, willing to sacrifice for the good of the relationship.

**Let's do this together**

Co-production, the phenomenon whereby businesses involve customers in the production of services, is here to stay. As technological advancements continue, customers will become more and more involved in serving themselves. However, researchers have warned of some pitfalls with co-production. In a study titled *"Psychological Implication of Customer Participation in Co-Production,"* published in the January 2003 edition of the Journal of Marketing, Dr. Neeli Bendapudi and Dr. Robert P. Leone discussed the psychological concept of "self-serving bias." This refers to the tendency for people working with others to take all the praise when things go well and to blame the other party when things do not go well. In other words, when customers experience bad service in a co-production scenario, they will tend to blame and even resent the company, while taking all the credit for any problem-free experience. The solution to this problem is simple. "Develop a strong bond with the customer first." In other words, let the customer fall in love with you first. According to the study, self-serving bias is less likely if customers feel they have a "romantic relationship with the business rather than just a business relationship.

**Cost doesn't really matter**

How many times have you disregarded the cost implications of a purchase just because it was for a loved one? When it comes to love, cost does not really matter. It has been found out that customers in love demonstrate less price sensitivity than less committed customers. When the romance is very deep between a company and its cherished customers, the committed customers will still prefer to do business with it no matter how difficult or more costly it is as compared to doing business with a competitor.

**Give me some more**

Customers in love are very profitable for the organisations they are in love with. These are the repeat buyers who the business can always trust to buy not once or twice but more often. True-hearted customers return more and more often, since they enjoy the service they receive from these firms. If your loved one is truly enthralled by your love, you can be sure he or she will keep coming back for more of your love.

## Anything new?

For those who have enjoyed a good offering from you, it is not too difficult for them to try new offerings. If customers are happy with what they have bought from you before, they will be more willing to try new products. Perhaps they will even trust you to suggest products suitable for them. Committed customers may sometimes come to you only to see if you have any new products on offer. Cross-selling is easier with already established customers.

## Customer-Evangelists

This is one of the main reasons why I believe all serious-minded business people should go out of their way to win the hearts of their customers. Customers in love can become the business' most effective marketing tool (far more trustworthy than salesmen in the eyes of other customers) and their services are free. These customers boast about the special treatment they are getting from you thereby enticing other good customers! They are evangelists for the business, preaching the gospel to others and "winning souls" for the organisation. Satisfied customers will generate referral business for you. They will gladly send their friends and family to you.

*". . . it will not suffice to have customers that are merely satisfied. Satisfied customers switch, for no good reason, just to try something else. Why not? Profit and growth come from customers*

*that can boast about your product or service—the loyal customer. He requires no advertising or other persuasion, and he brings a friend along with him."*

(W. Edwards Deming, American consultant*)*

I will forever cherish the moments when all I did in a day was to wait in the office and receive visitors who had been directed to me by my cherished customers. I remember a day I paid a visit to a customer I had very good relations with. As I entered his office I saw him having a chat with another gentleman. Immediately he saw me he exclaimed to his business partner, *"Yes, this is the gentleman I was just telling you about. He is such a great relations officer. You have to do business with him."* I walked out of that meeting with a new account. Thanks to the customer-evangelistic ministry of my cherished customer.

**You are my all**

This is the point where all companies should strive to get to with all their cherished customers. This is the stage where customers have so much trust in the company that they will not even go to the trouble of even trying out new competitors. When customers reach this point in the romance, they will not only make it a point to tell all of their friends, family and associates how great you are, but will take anything you say as the "gospel truth"!

This is what customers who are completely sold on your offering do. These are the customers who will never settle for an alternative, even when your product is not on the shelf. They will prefer to wait for yours, rather than try something else.

# CHAPTER 17
## *THE FINAL TOUCH*

*I never really understood the epilogue of a book. I've always figured that if an author needed additional room to make a point, she would just add another chapter.*

(Wil Schroter, author of *GO BIG or GO HOME*)

Taking Mr. Schroter's advice I am adding this chapter to make my final point. Studies estimate that some businesses can lose up to 40% of customers in a single year. This figure could be higher in Africa and some other parts of world with increasing competition from both local and global players. Businesses are in truly tough times. Customers are becoming more sophisticated by the day. They demand more value, are more technology-savvy and are more conscious of their rights as consumers.

Businesses have tried, and are still trying, many ways by which they can keep their best customers. New product-service offerings are being innovated and brought into the market as quickly as practicable. Sales and Marketing strategists are coming up with novel ways to get these innovative product-service offerings into the hands of end-users. Technological advancements are making business operations smoother. The Information and Communication Technology breakthroughs have revolutionalised the ways businesses operate.

However, it must be stated that no business has an absolute monopoly over all these ways and means. Fierce competitors can also find the right product at the right price, and can use a whole arsenal of means to entice customers to switch companies. Business leaders are faced with a daunting task as to what to do to keep their most valuable customers. To survive in these times, business leaders must direct their attention at the most important person in the business universe—the customer. The customer must be central to all the actions of the business, from what is produced, what its value is to how the product is placed in the customer's hands.

The fable is told of a young cloud that was born somewhere over the great Mediterranean. As it migrated with its folks towards the forest regions of Africa, it passed over a desert. As it gazed down, it saw a beautiful sand dune. It instantly fell in love with the golden sand dune. He decided to stay behind, against the wishes of his peers. They told him that it was not needed in the desert. Not one to be deterred, the cloud struck up a conversation with the dune.

"Tell me, how does it feel like down there?" he asked the dune.

The dune answered in a sad voice, "So and so. I have the company of the other dunes and the occasional caravans that pass by. Mine is a short life. Immediately the wind blows, I am gone."

The young cloud continued, "I have a similar story. Although I get to travel and see places, I will reach the tropical rain forest soon and then I would have to give up my rain and die."

"It seems we both do not have much to live for. But do you know what we call your rain here in the desert?" asked the sand dune.

"No. Tell me," demanded the young cloud.

"Paradise." said the dune. "Older dunes say it used to be so beautiful but I have never experienced this paradise before."

"Wow! I never knew my rain was so important. If you wouldn't mind I would give you my rain," said the cloud.

"But you would die," remarked the dune.

"I don't mind dying if it is to show you that I love you. As a matter of fact, my older folks tell me that love actually never dies. It is only transformed," came the reply from the cloud.

"I love you too."

The young cloud began to gradually shower the dune with its water. They stayed together for a while until the young cloud finally disappeared from the clouds. However, the next day the sand dune was covered with some grass, flowers and shrub. It was so beautiful. As other clouds that were headed to the forest passed by, they thought the patch of vegetation was a part of the rain forest. They each gave it some rain and before long, the entire region had become an oasis with trees and a stream that refresh all who passed by. Travellers who pass by never know that the beauty they behold and appreciate was all because one young cloud decided to, not only fall in love but, go a step further and give of itself to make a change.

I hope you are the young cloud. Customer Romance is about taking a stance against the norm. It is about deciding to do something that might not be necessarily beneficial in the present. If you would decide to go out there and not only preach but also practise the concept of Customer Romance, I am sure you will be amazed at how far your actions will go. Your business will flourish, your fame will spread and all who pass by will be naturally drawn to you. This is the power of the new feel of customer service—Customer Romance!

## ENDORSEMENTS FOR "CUSTOMER ROMANCE"

- *"J. N. Halm's Customer Romance is a unique, deeply felt, and very inspiring work on touching customers in a way that builds your bottom-line success."*

  Micah Solomon, customer service keynote speaker and consultant, author of *High-Tech, High-Touch Customer Service-USA*

- *Fantastic book. Jerry takes everyday customer concepts and masterfully plots a romantic relationship with customers. Every business executive needs this book".*

  Caleb Ayiku, Corporate Trainer & Founder, Breakthrough Consult-Ghana

- *Mr. Halm never ceases to excite me with his unique style of writing. He writes in such a way that the message sinks in without any difficulty. CUSTOMER ROMANCE takes the reader into uncharted territories without losing sight of the importance of the message. It's exciting . . . . Highly recommended.*

  Mike Nyinaku, Chief Executive Officer, Beige Group of Companies-Ghana

- *In today's competitive market which is also filled with a lot of broken promises, Jerry Halm's maiden book "Customer Romance" with the tag line "A new feel of customer service" is the real deal. He writes with passion and drive. Indeed he walks the talk and does it with deep and robust insight.*

Kwabena Agyekum, Executive Director, Chartered Institute Of Marketing, Ghana

- *After years of consistently churning out some of the most exciting weekly articles on service experience management, it is not a surprise that J. N. Halm has finally come out with this masterpiece. CUSTOMER ROMANCE is a must read for all who intend to stay in business for long.*

William Selassy Adjadogo, Editor, *Business and Financial Times,* Ghana

- *The comparison of the customer and client relationship with metaphorical undertones to a seemingly involved relationship creates an ambience for an adventurous and enjoyable read.*

Gregory Eid, Managing Director, TeleData ICT, Ghana

- *The mantra that "the customer is king" requires kingly blueprints for superior customer service and I have now discovered a book by no other person than J. N. Halm that exactly deals with this subject matter. You need this book as an individual or a business for survival!*

George Kojo Addison, Managing Director, StarLife Assurance Co. Limited, Ghana

- *Customer service is easy to talk about and harder to deliver. For too many, it is an elusive concept. Mr. Jerry Halm has captured the essence of outstanding customer service. After reading this book, one could develop a winning customer service program. His use of storytelling is powerfully utilized to cement the concept into our consciousness. "Customer Romance" is full of "golden nuggets" of information and it is easy to read. I would recommend it for anyone who is interested in customer service.*

**Glen N. Jones** (President & COO, Main Street Management Group, USA and former Verizon Communication, Inc. executive)

---

הבהא אוה םיהולא

1 John 4:8

www.ingramcontent.com/pod-product-compliance
Lightning Source LLC
Chambersburg PA
CBHW030812180526
45163CB00003B/1246

*9 7 8 1 4 9 1 8 9 6 7 8 5 *